HOW TO BECOME A TAI CHI TEACHER

7 Practical Steps Towards Setting Up a Class of Your Own

by

Colin and Gaynel Hamilton

The 7 Steps Towards Mastery Series Volume 3

Disclaimer

The authors of this book are not responsible, in any manner whatsoever, for any damage or injury of any kind that may result from practicing or applying the principles, ideas or techniques described in this book. As with any other type of unaccustomed exercise, readers are advised to consult a doctor before embarking on any kind of martial arts training.

ISBN: 9781982986131

For Bob France

Acknowledgements

We would like to express our gratitude to our own teachers: Dr. Zhu Guang, Robert France, Dr. Chen Haifeng, Nigel Sutton, Ray Wilkie, Michael Tse, and Master Tan Ching Ngee; to others whom we consider to be great teachers, including Bob Lowey, Christina Bunney and Grandmaster Chen Xiaowang, and also to our Tai Chi ancestors, especially Yang Lu Chan, Yang Jian Ho, Tien Zhaolin, Yang Cheng Fu, Liu Dequan, Professor Cheng Man Ching, and Professor Wang Zhizhong.

We would also like to thank Barbara Doyle and Ben Bisco, who have kindly proof-read our manuscript and provided helpful feedback during the production process; Zoë Hamilton for her invaluable guidance on the cover design; John Donegan for asking us to include a catalogue of the enrichment exercises that we use in our own classes (which turned out to be an important section of this book), and to Bob and Noreen Weatherall at the BCCMA for their friendship and support for many years.

Not least, we thank our thousands of students and training partners, past and present. We especially appreciate the efforts of all of those who have undergone our instructor training programme and contributed to its evolution and development as they went on to become instructors in their own right. It has been our privilege to share our art with such an enthusiastic, committed and inspiring group of people.

Most of all, we would like to thank our children for putting up with our Tai Chi all these years and for their unwavering confidence in our ability to get these books finished eventually. Thanks guys!

Contents

Other Books in the 7 Steps Towards Mastery Series

Volume 1

How to Move Towards Tai Chi Mastery; 7 Practical Steps to Improve Your Tai Chi Forms and Access Your Internal Power

Volume 2

How to Use Tai Chi for Self-defence: 7 Practical Steps to Develop Your Martial Skills and Avoid Having to Use Them

Introduction

Those Who Can, Teach!

The moment you live something, you are teaching it

whether you want to or not.

Dadi Janki

What is it about Tai Chi that has inspired you to think about teaching it? Have you noticed, perhaps, that Tai Chi can change people's lives? Has your own life been so enriched by practicing Tai Chi that you are now passionate about helping others to share that experience?

Maybe there are so many reasons that it's difficult to list them all, but maybe those reasons include wanting to:

- help people to stay healthy, happy and mobile throughout their lives,

- help people to discover a meditative practice with the capacity to calm minds, enhance spiritual awareness and perhaps even reduce conflict in these uncertain times,

- help people to learn how to protect themselves, or

- help to pass on authentic Tai Chi so that it doesn't fade into distant memory.

If any or all of these apply to you, but you are not sure how to go about setting up a class of your own, then you are the person we are writing this book for.

We would like to help you to get started as a teacher by sharing with you all the things we wished we had known when we first set out to teach Tai Chi, so that you don't have to learn those lessons the hard way!

We will assume that you are good at Tai Chi but new to teaching and we will take a step-by-step approach so that you can gradually build the skills and confidence you need to go it alone.

If you are teaching already, there may still be some interesting tips or information in this book that make a perusal of its contents worth your time. In fact the final chapter was written with experienced teachers in mind, as a source of inspiration if you would like to enrich the learning experience of your students, consider the various levels of their development and reflect upon the artistry involved in teaching Tai Chi.

Who is this book for?

In summary then, this book is for you if:

- You are already a skilled and knowledgeable Tai Chi Practitioner of an authentic style of Tai Chi, and

- You have a real desire to share your skills and knowledge with other people and you would like some advice on how go about it, or

- You have started teaching Tai Chi already but, as a reflective practitioner, you are open to useful suggestions and information.

If you have the best of motives for teaching but you are not already a skilled and knowledgeable Tai Chi practitioner, then obviously that training needs to come first and we hope you will hold on to your enthusiasm and passion for Tai Chi while you continue your studies with a competent instructor and perhaps gain some teaching experience as you go, by assisting in their classes. We have written other books to support you with the actual process of learning Tai Chi. In this book, we will not be looking at how to do Tai Chi, only how to teach it.

What we would urge you to avoid, however, is signing up for an 'instructor training programme' with a teacher you don't know, either in the flesh or online, who insists that you don't need any previous experience of Tai Chi at all and promises to make you a 'qualified instructor' after only a few weeks! This is blatantly impossible and you will come away with an unenviable hotchpotch of questionable skills and probably a second mortgage on your house!

Whether you are hoping to teach the full martial art of Tai Chi Chuan, or whether you have chosen to teach it for health and relaxation only, we suggest that, as a minimum, you need to be practicing an authentic style in a way that follows all of the accepted Tai Chi principles and is safe and unlikely to cause injury to yourself and others.

If you are not sure about the authenticity of the style you are teaching, check your lineage if you can. You might also compare what you are doing with YouTube videos of some of the great Tai Chi practitioners out there in the main styles such as Chen, Yang, Wu, Hao, Sun and Chen Man Ching styles or the Beijing 24 step, 48 step or 42 step competition style. There are lots of differences of interpretation, even within a particular family style, but all of these diverse forms should obey the Tai Chi principles, as described in the Tai Chi Classics, and be recognisable as Tai Chi, rather than a qigong set or a made-up form of exercise.

As a rule of thumb, if your style includes arching your back and sticking out your bottom behind you, locking your arms out straight, wiggling your hips and leaning in various directions, over-bending your knees so that when you walk forwards your front knee goes beyond your toes, or lifting your shoulders and elbows level with your ears, you have a very good reason to question its authenticity.

You don't have to be a fully-fledged master to teach Tai Chi. All of us are forever on a steep learning curve, yet however far along it we are, we may have a helping hand to offer those who tread the path behind us.

Who are we?

We are a married couple who have been teaching Tai Chi for over three decades. We have trained fighters and we have trained instructors and, most importantly, we have seen how Tai Chi has helped thousands of our students to improve their health, mobility and quality of life.

Teaching Tai Chi is not the easiest profession in this world but, in our opinion, it can be one of the most satisfying. We hope that we can help you to share the immense pleasure that we have found in teaching Tai Chi.

How can we help you?

We are not for one moment suggesting that what you will read in these pages is the only way to go about teaching Tai Chi. We are simply offering, with great respect for other teachers out there, what we have learned from our own experience, in the hope that you might find it useful. This book is intended as a friendly guide at your side rather than an authoritative instruction manual. In the end, you will find your own approach to teaching: a way that works best for you and your students.

Our own approach was undoubtedly influenced by the valuable lessons we learned at the feet of some excellent teachers over many years and it has subsequently developed further as we have explored what works best to suit the needs of our own students.

We are both science graduates with post graduate teaching qualifications and many years of experience in the field of adult education. We have worked as judges in international competitions and as assessors and verifiers for national awarding bodies, and we have even written some national qualifications.

So we know all about the jargon and paperwork that can be so off-putting when you first enter the teaching profession. We will try to keep this book jargon-free while at the same time sharing with you everything you need to know about good professional practice, wherever you find yourself teaching.

If you can, teach!

There are many excellent Tai Chi practitioners in this world. There are also many brilliant teachers. Finding an excellent Tai Chi practitioner who is also willing and able to teach, however, can be a real challenge.

In the past, valuable skills and knowledge may have been lost when lineage holders lacked the desire, ability or patience to communicate their hard-won expertise to more than a handful of students, if any, while less talented individuals had the charisma to attract crowds of followers.

More worryingly, whenever Tai Chi enjoys a surge in popularity, it tends to attract a crowd of exercise teachers who are more than ready to jump on the bandwagon but less enthusiastic about finding out what Tai Chi actually is, resulting in some weirdly unrecognisable inventions that not only mislead their unwary students but potentially damage them in the process.

We hope that, by writing this book, we can encourage and assist some good Tai Chi people to become great teachers and pass on the art to future generations.

Of course, no book can ever be a substitute for the experience gained from actual teaching. Nothing boosts your learning curve faster than the need to show and explain your skills to someone else, helping them to overcome any difficulties on the way, so that they can eventually do it too. Therefore, this book is designed to support and compliment your actual practice of teaching.

In our own school, our trainee instructors assist us in our classes, in various settings, while they gather evidence of their teaching skills until they are competent and confident enough to teach classes on their own.

So help in class if you can. We know of many good teachers out there who provide instructor training for their advanced students and allow them to help out in class as a matter of course; eventually granting some of them permission to become instructors in their own right. This is standard practice in most martial arts schools. We hope that you already have such a teacher and you are able to gain some teaching experience by assisting your fellow students in their classes. Our guide will then become a means of looking more deeply at what you are doing and what you need to consider before you go it alone.

If you don't have an opportunity to help in anyone else's classes at the moment, you might be able to teach a few moves to family and friends so that they can benefit from your efforts as you 'find your feet' as a teacher.

If you are already teaching on your own, you might still find this book helpful as a source of ideas, such as the 'enrichment' activities that we have included in the final chapter. It might also provide an opportunity to reflect on your practice, particularly if you are working in an establishment where your lessons are observed by various inspectors and you want to be prepared for those visits. The time you spend studying this book may also count towards your continuous professional development (CPD) portfolio.

What you will find in this book

The information we will share with you in this step-by-step guide will include practical advice on:

- Why your students are there and how you can help them to get what they came for;
- The records you need to keep (and those you shouldn't);
- How to teach Tai Chi safely;
- How to pass on the art effectively and hone your skills as you go along;
- How to plan your lessons and courses without getting too bogged down in the paperwork;
- How to survive (and possibly thrive on) official inspections!
- What legal and professional requirements you need to consider, including licences and insurance;
- Where and how to set up classes. You might, for example, hire a hall or work in schools, colleges, community centres, care homes or health clubs. We will be looking at the pros and cons of each of these to help you to decide where best to accommodate your own students.

- At the end of some sections we will provide questions to ask yourself so that you can check your understanding of key points and their relevance to what you are doing.

All of this involves putting the needs of the students first.

Teaching is not about teachers; it is about the people they teach. With this in mind, you will naturally become a great teacher.

Really great teachers are not measured by their expertise in a particular subject or by their ability to attract students and establish a reputation, they are there to help people to meet their various needs and discover their full potential. We want to help you to become a really great teacher. In the process, you might improve the quality of countless lives and facilitate the development of masters.

Step 1

Put Your Students First

This section is all about the needs and rights of your students. If you understand and respect these needs and rights, then you are likely to be a great teacher and all the professional requirements we discuss later will appear to be a simple matter of common sense.

What Do People Need?

People go along to Tai Chi classes for many different reasons, only one of which is to study the subject they signed up for. As a teacher, you need to have some idea of what it was that brought them through your door and then do your very best to provide them with a learning experience that will help them to find whatever it is that they need, whether that is to learn how to protect themselves, or to help them to recover from a hip replacement operation, or simply as an opportunity to meet other people and make some friends.

However valid these reasons seem to you; for each person, they are important enough to have got them out of the house and into your training hall and, just by being aware of these, you can ensure that you tailor your classes to meet the individual needs of every person present.

You can't possibly know what all of those needs are for every person you meet and we certainly do not recommend subjecting each of your students to some kind of psychological interrogation to discover their deepest hopes and fears!

What you can have, however, is an awareness of the needs common to all human beings; which will allow you to set up a learning environment in which most individuals will thrive.

Let's start by looking at what types of needs human beings have that might be accommodated in your classes.

Three useful models of human needs are:

- Maslow's Hierarchy of Human Needs
- The SPIES model
- The Human Givens Model

They all tend to say the same things, since they are all describing the needs of all human beings, but they offer different ways of remembering them.

Maslow's Hierarchy of Human Needs

Abraham Maslow was a guy who turned psychology on its head by looking at what makes a person healthy, balanced and happy, rather than at what makes them depressed, anxious and ill. He found that people who appeared to have life well and truly sorted tended to have several things in common and he arranged these in a triangle or pyramid, with the most basic needs at the bottom, building the others on top of them, layer by layer.

He began with the absolute basics, the physical needs of every individual. Without air, food, water, sleep and warmth, we wouldn't last very long and all our other needs would be irrelevant. He then reasoned that, even with all these basic needs taken care of, we wouldn't be particularly healthy if we were living on the street in fear of being attacked by muggers or worse, so safety and security came next.

After that came relationships: the emotional need to be with other people; to love and to be loved. He also saw that all of this is pointless if we don't value ourselves, so self-esteem was the next crucial factor. Being respected and valued by others contributes to one's own sense of self-worth. Having self-esteem is not the same as being selfish or building ourselves an ego; it just means being comfortable with ourselves and getting rid of any negative views and feelings we may have about the way we are.

With all of these layers in place, the stage is set for the final point of the triangle: self-actualization. This is all about the achievement of our full potential and the fulfilment of our highest needs, including the need to understand the universe we live in and our place within it. We need opportunities to learn and to appreciate beautiful things as well as to set and achieve our own goals, be creative, pursue our hobbies and interests and follow our own chosen 'spiritual path'.

All of these factors are interdependent. Without self-esteem, for example, we might be less likely to go out and form satisfying relationships with others, less likely to find employment and therefore less able to earn money to provide for our basic security and physical needs. Take one rung from the ladder and the whole thing tends to collapse.

If there are bits of our triangle missing, that is often where any stress or ill health is coming from, and that is often the point where we can to start to put things right.

Simply by providing a regular weekly Tai Chi class, we have an opportunity to help others to improve their physical health and mobility, learn how to protect themselves, cope with stress, establish new relationships, increase their confidence and self-esteem, and perhaps find more meaning in their lives. We can help people to rebuild their pyramids!

The SPIES Model

This model is often used in the training of teachers and carers.

S.P.I.E.S. stands for Social, Physical, Intellectual, Emotional and Spiritual.

The model can be used to represent either human needs or the various aspects of human growth and development. The categories echo those of Maslow's triangle but in a way that is perhaps easier to remember.

It is useful for Tai Chi teachers because it reminds us of the various reasons that students may have for attending classes. When teaching a class of twenty people it is easy to work to our own personal teaching agenda and forget that there are twenty individuals present, with at least twenty different reasons for being there.

These individual needs can vary hugely and each person may be seeking to meet several needs at the same time, whether they are aware of that or not. In just one class there may be people who want to learn to protect themselves while others just want to learn to relax or be able to sleep better. Some may have been referred by their doctor or have heard that Tai Chi is good for arthritis or asthma or a heart condition, or that it can help to relieve their back pain, or improve their balance, their memory or their posture. Recent research has also revealed distinct benefits for people suffering from Parkinson's Disease and Fibromyalgia and studies worldwide have shown that regular practice can reduce the risk of falling.

Potentially, Tai Chi can help with all of these needs and many more, but a lot depends on the teacher, how aware they are of the needs of individuals and how they relate to those individuals and structure their class to accommodate these needs. So let's have a look at how you can do this.

Social Needs

Students may have come along to your class because they are feeling lonely and isolated and want an opportunity to meet other people and perhaps to gain confidence and improve their social skills. The friendly 'family' atmosphere of a Tai Chi class, where everyone shares similar interests, can provide an excellent opportunity for this. As a teacher, you can help by making everyone feel welcome and allowing people time to talk to each other. This might be by:

- Having a short refreshment break in the middle, if possible.

- Getting people to work together in small groups.

- Allowing new starters to spend some time with a more experienced student, perhaps a different one each week, so that they get to know several people in the class quite well.

A lonely person might walk into an aerobics class, do the routines and walk out again without speaking to anyone and still be as lonely as ever when they leave. If they enter a Tai Chi class, we would hope that, by the end of the session, they will have made at least one friend.

Physical Needs

We know that, as a form of exercise, Tai Chi benefits all parts of the body, from muscles and bones to the heart, brain, lungs and circulation. Many students might have come to you on the recommendation of their doctor or physiotherapist. As teachers, our role is to teach Tai Chi as accurately and safely as possible so that our students have a chance to experience the benefits and don't end up going out with more problems than they came in with.

Sleep is also a physical need and our Tai Chi students often tell us that, as well as feeling generally calmer during the day, they also tend to sleep better since they took up Tai Chi. This could be significant because recent research has shown that, during a night of deep and restful sleep, long-term memories are laid down and a kind of clean up and repair process goes on in the brain. During the deepest levels of sleep, brain cells actually shrink so that cerebrospinal fluid can wash away any waste products that have built up during the day, such as the amyloid proteins that might otherwise stick around – literally – to form the plaques associated with Alzheimer' disease.

Another aspect we can help with is the need for physical safety and security. Teaching the martial aspects of Tai Chi might help a person to develop the skills to be able to defend themselves effectively in some situations, and you might also be able to offer advice on how to avoid dangerous situations in the first place.

You will need to tread a fine line here, however. Try to avoid making your students so over-confident in their skills that they take unnecessary risks (which can be a problem with martial arts training generally) but do be careful not to make them so paranoid that they are afraid to go out to their cars after the class!

Intellectual Needs

Human beings have an innate need to learn new things and stretch themselves intellectually. Tai Chi provides this opportunity. In fact, according to the results of a study published in the Journal of Alzheimer's Disease, it has actually been shown to increase the size of the brains of practitioners! For this reason, it is now recommended by the Alzheimer's Society. You can help with this intellectual stimulation by explaining the Tai Chi principles and applications as you go along, rather than just getting people to copy your movements in silence all the time. Having said that, it's important not to fall into the habit of always 'talking them through it'. The student eventually has to let go of any attempts to understand Tai Chi intellectually and enter the stage of their journey where they can do the form without thinking, so that they can experience it fully. Even silent practice of a sequence may help to grow the hippocampus, an area associated with spatial awareness, which has been shown to be particularly well-developed in London taxi drivers.

Emotional Needs

These are explored in much more depth in the next section, where we look at the Human Givens model, but in general, people need to feel a sense of belonging to something bigger than themselves and to feel valued and cared for. This doesn't mean being overly affectionate and encouraging lots of hugging in each class. A friendly smile, a kind word and an overall ethos of equality and respect can help someone to feel welcome and at home. If you genuinely care about your students, this tends to happen naturally.

As well as helping people to feel better, the calming and meditative aspects of Tai Chi may have wider implications for the health and well-being of practitioners. Recent studies have shown that practices such as Tai Chi, qigong and meditation can actually reduce inflammation in the body by reducing the activity of the genes that are associated with inflammation. Why is that a good thing? Because inflammation is known to give rise to a whole swathe of health problems from heart disease, stroke and rheumatoid arthritis to Alzheimer's Disease, diabetes and cancer, so Tai Chi is finally becoming mainstream, in terms of the recognition of its potential medical benefits, and the need for competent teachers is likely to increase.

Spiritual Needs

If you were to ask a thousand people what the word 'spiritual' means to them, you would probably get a thousand different answers and some would just not have a clue where to start. We therefore use this word very carefully. Spiritual needs can range from appreciation of beauty to personal fulfilment, happiness or a feeling that life has meaning, and Tai Chi has been known to help with all of these things.

Tai Chi is not a religion and no one has to be a Taoist to do it, yet it does contain a rich philosophy that can help people to find a depth to life that makes some kind of sense of the world around them. Its mindful, meditative aspects can reduce anxiety and perhaps enable them to find some peace.

However, though many students may be attracted to Tai Chi for emotional or spiritual comfort, do take care not to allow yourself to be seen as some kind of wise and all-knowing guru! That can become a slippery slope indeed!

The Human Givens Model

'Human Givens' is just a name for the needs and resources we are born with. The following lists were compiled by Joe Griffin and Ivan Tyrrell; the founders of the Human Givens Institute.

Our emotional needs

Whenever our emotional needs are not met, or when our resources are being used in unhelpful ways, we suffer considerable distress; and so can those around us.

According to the Human Givens Institute, our fundamental emotional needs are:

- security (safe territory and an environment which allows us to develop well);

- attention – to give and receive it;
- a sense of autonomy and control;
- feeling part of a wider community;
- emotional intimacy – to know that at least one other person accepts us totally for who we are, 'warts and all';
- a sense of status within social groupings;
- a sense of competence and achievement (which comes from successful learning and effectively applying skills – an antidote to ‘low self-esteem’);
- privacy (an opportunity to reflect on and consolidate our experiences);
- a sense of meaning and purpose (which can come from being ‘stretched’ in what we do and think).

If we reflect on each of the above in turn, we can see that, potentially, a Tai Chi class can help many people to meet some or all of these needs. Sometimes, it is like a domino effect; just being there and providing a welcoming environment, in which people can meet other people and learn a short sequence, can have a knock-on effect of boosting their self-esteem and enabling them to feel part of a wider community.

This may give them enough confidence to spend more time with other people outside the class, thereby creating more opportunities for emotional intimacy, more autonomy and more control over their lives as a whole. It may even help them to discover more meaning and purpose in their lives.

If this seems to be an exaggerated claim, we have students in their eighties and nineties who are active, optimistic and still enjoying Tai Chi. In contrast, we could give you many examples of older people who have experienced various physical and mental health problems as a result of many years of inactivity and loneliness. We can only wonder what a difference it might have made to their quality of life if they had been able to get to a regular Tai Chi class.

The aim is NOT to create an ongoing dependence on the class or the teacher, - do take great care not to allow your school to become some kind of cult - but to create a supportive and welcoming environment in which people are able to discover and draw upon their own natural resources in order to meet their own needs.

Our innate resources

Fortunately, most of us were also born with considerable resources that we can use to meet our own needs. You can find a more detailed list of these innate resources on the website of the Human Givens Institute but here are a few examples of those strengths and how Tai Chi can allow us to use and develop them.

- We have a rational brain that we can use to solve problems, ask questions, analyse and plan, and we have the ability to develop and use long-term memory. Learning a complex Tai

Chi sequence, as we have seen, can actually cause the brain to grow and has been shown to improve cognitive function.

- We have the ability to build rapport, empathise and connect with other people. Research has shown that moving with others in a synchronised way can create empathy and rapport within and between groups of people, from marching soldiers to formation dancers, so performing a Tai Chi sequence in a class may be expected to contribute to a person's sense of belongingness and connectedness.

- We have an imagination which, when used constructively, can help us to visualise and create our future and we have the ability to dream and to understand through metaphor. The power of imagination and metaphor can be used very effectively to enable students to learn the more subtle aspects of Tai Chi. From time to time it's useful to mention the ones from the Tai Chi Classics, such as 'flowing like a river', 'gliding serenely on the wind like an eagle' or drawing in the arms 'like the delicate reeling in of silk'. Ultimately, the Tai Chi form itself can be used as a metaphor for life, as you will see from the final chapter of this book when we discuss the spontaneous state and the wave analogy.

- We have a sense of self-awareness - an 'observing self' - that allows us to step back and notice the content of our own minds and, if necessary, change it. We can take a wider viewpoint and see things in a clearer perspective. This is one of the great benefits of practicing Tai Chi and meditation. Tai Chi can be seen as a kind of mindful meditation practice which can help people to switch at will from the 'doing' mode

> of thinking - which can lead to excessive introspection and rumination, especially at night, causing disturbed sleep patterns and depression - to the 'being' mode of thinking in which the mind can simply rest in the moment and appreciate it fully. Tai Chi therefore allows people an opportunity to experience life in the present for a while, rather than going over regrets from the past or worries about the future and frantically searching for ways to 'fix everything'.

Many of your students will be largely content, resourceful and already meeting their needs effectively, but others may benefit considerably from discovering and developing their own innate resources.

All of this may sound a little over-ambitious for a mere Tai Chi class but in practice, it is extremely common for students to report improvements in their health and well-being, mentally and physically, within weeks of starting to learn Tai Chi. Typically, people say that they are sleeping better, have more energy, feel calmer, more relaxed, more in control and generally happier.

While you will always need to be aware of the needs of your students, however long they have been with you, the most obvious point at which you will need to consider this is when they first turn up at your class.

Getting to Know Your Students

A student's first lesson is often the most important, as this will be the point where they form their first opinions of your class and of you as a teacher. Although, with the best will in the world, you can't please everyone all the time, a planned reception for new students can increase the possibility that they will see it as a positive experience.

You will need to find out several things about your new students early on and it is worth considering how you will go about this. When you are an experienced instructor you may allocate this responsibility to an assistant instructor or you may make a point of doing it yourself. Either way, a friendly greeting can make a newcomer feel welcome and simply introducing yourself and asking a few relevant but not overly personal questions can help you to determine:

- Whether they are in the right class: “Hi. Are you here for the Tai Chi class?”

- Why they are there: “What attracted you to Tai Chi?”

- What previous experience they have, if any, and what further training they will need: “Have you done any Tai Chi before?”

- Whether they have any health problems which might make part of your training unsuitable for them: “Are you feeling fit and well at the moment?”

From this first brief, informal conversation, you may also gain some idea of their expectations and perhaps let them know a bit about what goes on in your class. At some stage during their first lesson, you, or an assistant instructor, will need to go on to tell them a little about what Tai Chi is all about and perhaps provide advice on suitable clothing and any health and safety requirements.

You can also let them know about your school website, if you have one, where they can find more information and begin to get a feel for the overall ethos of the school and the opportunities it provides, and perhaps begin to feel part of a wider community.

If you have a large number of new students starting together, you might provide a brief questionnaire for them to fill in and a leaflet with essential information about Tai Chi and about you and your class/school.

This can save a lot of time but there may be students present who cannot read or write, or whose first language is different from yours. Being faced with the task of reading and writing when they come along to a class for physical exercise can be very off-putting and even frightening for some people, so be flexible and don't insist that everyone has to fill in a questionnaire.

You can gain the same information by chatting with the group, asking for people to put their hands up if they have done Tai Chi before and suggesting that anyone with concerns about their health can speak to you privately during the break.

All of this can be time consuming and if you have new students starting nearly every week, you may need to devise very efficient ways of accomplishing the task without taking up too much lesson time and disadvantaging your regular students.

However well you organise your induction process, a potentially frustrating aspect of teaching can be the weekly arrival of new beginners who need lots of personal attention and then decide it's not for them and never come back. This is almost inevitable, as many people hear about Tai Chi and come along out of curiosity then find it's not for them, so don't take it personally and feel that you have failed in some way for not maintaining their interest. The record for us was two young girls who came in late, wearing leotards and carrying yoga mats, while we were holding a stationary qigong posture. They stood with us for a half a minute and then went out again and later commented that the class was "not aerobic enough"!

All you can do is lay out your wares and expect that many of your customers will be window-shopping or browsing and will go away again very quickly if the 'vibe' is not what they were looking for.

Often, it's not anything you did that put them off. It could just be work pressure or family commitments or any one of a thousand other reasons. That student may come back to you, or to another Tai Chi class, when their children are at school or they retire from full-time work.

Even if they never return, they may have had a pleasant experience and, for some, that may have planted a seed that will lie dormant for a few years and then grow into a deeper interest. We once had someone come along who said: "I went to a maths lesson of yours once and you did a meditation at the beginning to calm us all down. I went home and taught it to my sister, who used it to overcome her fear of flying. I've come back to thank you and see what else I can learn from you."

One solution to the challenge of coping with weekly new starters is to have a beginner's class plus an intermediate class for those who stick with it. Another suggestion is to have a waiting list with specific entry dates for beginners. Such solutions may not always be possible, however, due to financial considerations or insufficient student numbers, and there is always the risk that people on a waiting list may lose interest and give up or go elsewhere. We aim not to turn anyone away. That one person could be the one with the potential to become a great master, or the one who was desperately needing your class as a first step towards turning their life around.

In any case, all classes are 'mixed ability'. Even if you have several classes at various levels, whatever the general level of the class you are teaching, every person in it will be an individual, working at their own pace and learning the art in different ways, so you will always need to structure your class in such a way that everyone receives the right amount of attention and is able to make some progress.

We will say more about how to do this later when we look in detail at lesson planning and how to structure a class but before we get on to the nitty-gritty of how to actually teach, we will spend a bit of time considering how to look after your students by supporting their rights, providing a safe and accessible learning environment and protecting their confidentiality.

What to Write Down

While there are things you need to know about your students, what you record in writing needs to be kept to a minimum, not just because writing things down is time-consuming and not what your students came to an exercise class for, but also because the recording of other people's private information is a huge responsibility and carries a risk of inadvertently breaching their right to confidentiality.

Confidentiality and Data Protection

As a Tai Chi instructor, it is almost inevitable that you will have access to some personal information about your students and you might need to write some of this down. A rule of thumb is to do this on a very strictly need-to-know basis. In the UK, anyone gathering and storing information about other people must comply with the requirements of the Data Protection Act and, from May 2018, the new General Data Protection Regulation (GDPR).

If it's not essential FOR THE STUDENT to have that information recorded by you, then don't write it down.

This includes requests from your employers to record what you believe to be unnecessary personal information about your students. This is particularly prevalent in medical settings, where you may be asked to write detailed reports on every student in order to continue to secure the funding for your class.

Some organisations may ask your students to fill in forms that include their age, weight, ethnicity, religion or other data that seems inappropriate. If you feel this is a violation of your student's right to privacy, then don't be afraid to challenge it.

The worst that could happen is that they hire a different teacher, or the class closes and you set up a different one elsewhere. The best that can happen is that the management reconsiders their strategy and takes a small step towards the support of human rights.

Having said that, as an absolute minimum, the one written record you do need to have for every class is a register.

Registers

A register of attendance is a legal document which could be used in a court of law to prove the whereabouts of an individual at a certain time.

It can also be used in a Health Club as a check that all non-members have paid at the desk and that your numbers tally with the cash taken at the till, which could cost a receptionist their job if there are discrepancies.

Even if there is no official requirement, it is wise to keep one in case there was a fire, a bomb scare or even a practice fire drill so that, when you assemble outside, the Fire Brigade knows if there is anyone left inside the building.

For these reasons, it is really important to complete them accurately and make sure you don't forget to record the person who came in late or slipped in at the back without you seeing them. A head count can be a good way to check that everyone has been marked present, unless one slipped out to the toilet while you were counting.

Some employers require you to complete your registers at the start of every class and leave them in a locked filing cabinet or cupboard on site. In private classes you need them for yourself, and for your tax records, as proof of who has paid.

Although most registers will be physical paper documents, some colleges now insist that, after the class, you complete an electronic version, which you access by logging on to a secure area of the college intranet.

Contact numbers

As well as names and dates of attendance, it's also helpful to have a current contact number or email address for each student so that you can let them know if a class has to be cancelled. A College or Health Club will already have this information on file and an administrator will normally contact your students for you, but if it's your own private class you will need to keep the list at home or in your office, if you have one.

Licences

As a martial arts teacher, your students may need to be insured. We will come back to this later in the chapter on legal and professional requirements (Step 6) but it's worth mentioning here that you will need to keep a record of which students have current martial arts licences and their dates of renewal.

More personal information

Due to health and safety requirements, you will need to ask new students if they have any medical or other problems you should be aware of. Whether you do this in writing, as a questionnaire completed during the first class, or by informal discussion, you need to do it in a way which does not allow other people to overhear or oversee this information if your student wishes it to remain confidential.

Initial questionnaires should be shredded, once they have served their purpose of letting you know about any health issues, and that information should NOT be transferred onto a computer.

If a student does not wish to divulge any information about their health, this should be respected but any potential risks should be pointed out.

The nature of Tai Chi means that people are often drawn to it as a means of finding inner peace and relief from stress, therefore they may wish to confide in you and discuss personal problems. This raises issues of confidentiality as well as the question of whether or not you are the best person for them to be talking to or whether they would be better advised to seek the help of a professional therapist.

If they are just wanting to offload and chat to you as a friend, that's fine but some students may see you as some kind of guru or expert on all matters psychological and spiritual, just because you are a Tai Chi teacher! While you might find this flattering, it is very dangerous territory! The best you can do for them is to listen to what they are saying and, if you do offer advice, let them know that it is just your own personal opinion.

It may be that you have skills and training in this area and you are perfectly comfortable in dealing with such situations, or you may find that you are sometimes out of your depth and need to recommend that your student seeks help elsewhere, perhaps from their doctor or a reputable therapist. Or they may need practical or legal help from a Citizen's Advice Bureau or Social Services.

If there is a clear need for you to seek help on their behalf, for example if they are in danger of abuse, you will need to discuss this with them first rather than betray their trust by reporting your concerns without their agreement. Some organisations you may work for, especially universities, schools or colleges, may have company policies for such situations and you may have to attend a safeguarding course and be tested on your understanding of this process as part of the conditions of your contract of employment.

As well as keeping confidential information to yourself, you may also need to encourage students to be discreet and respectful towards one another, though in our experience there has never been a need for this, other than when teaching children.

With regard to the storage of data, we advise that no confidential information about your students should be kept on your home computer or external data storage device. Even with the best anti-virus software, computers can be hacked and storage devices can be mislaid so nothing should be on yours that could compromise the safety, security or privacy of your students.

In practice, the most information you might need to keep a record of in a database or spreadsheet would be the names, telephone numbers, email addresses and renewal dates for the individual martial arts licences/insurance of your students. This information should not be shared with anyone else. If someone asks for the contact details of a student, contact the student yourself and ask them to get in touch with the person making the enquiry, if they choose to. If this seems to be a bit over-protective, consider what might happen if your student had been relocated as part of a witness protection programme or was hiding from an abusive former partner. For the same reason, be very aware that a class photograph on your website or Facebook could breach someone's safety and security so never post a photo without permission and never share information about your students on social media.

You should never record their home addresses, medical information or financial information electronically. If they want to pay you for tuition fees, licences or products online, they can do that through a secure system like PayPal, so you never need to know their credit card details.

Any written information, such as the initial learner agreements required by some colleges, should normally be kept in a locked filing cabinet and a copy given to the student. These should not be left lying around for other students to see. Ideally, feedback sheets at the end of term should be anonymous, allowing students to be honest while also protecting their confidentiality.

In general, anything written down about any student should be kept to an absolute minimum wherever possible. When the need for information has expired, it should be shredded or, if digital, deleted.

An exception would be in a case where there is an incident which might lead to litigation, such as an accident or dispute. In such cases, accident/incident reports must be completed fully and signed by all parties, including witnesses, if possible, and these records are kept indefinitely. (If this seems a bit extreme, consider the case where an employee tried to sue her company for a disability arising from an injury to a finger and subsequent complications arising years later. The accident report, however, showed that the finger injured at work was a different finger on the opposite hand. The case was dismissed. So be very specific when recording injuries in such reports.)

Questions to ask yourself

- When a person comes to a Tai Chi class for the first time, what would you, the instructor, need to know about them? Why?

- In order to find out this information, what questions could you ask?

- Are there any questions you should not ask?

- Would it better for answers to these questions to be verbal or written down? What are the advantages and disadvantages of each?

- Apart from during initial assessment, when else might you need to remember confidentiality?

- When and how might you need to break confidentiality?

If you are required by an employer to use an initial assessment questionnaire with new students in a class:

- Where might you keep completed questionnaires?

- Who would need to see them?

- Where should they not be left?

- How long might you need to keep them?

- What details, if any, might you keep on a computer?

How to Keep the Playing Field Level

Unlike the traditional Eastern Tai Chi schools, where a teacher might send away newcomers until they have proved their worth, we make a point of welcoming whoever comes through our door unless they pose a real risk to the safety of others.

If you are setting up your own school, it would be a good idea to draw up your own equal opportunities statement, which all your students and instructors are expected to follow, such as:

No person shall be discriminated against, directly or indirectly, on the grounds of race, place of origin, class, caste, creed, culture, gender, marital status, mental ability, physical ability, sexuality, size, appearance, political beliefs, opinions or religion.

We reserve the right to refuse membership and/or tuition to, or withdraw it from, individuals guilty of gross misconduct, such as violent or aggressive behaviour, intimidation, sexual harassment, racism, or other behaviour likely to cause harm to any individual or bring the school into disrepute.

While, in general, Tai Chi is a gentle form of exercise, suitable for all ages and levels of ability and has been found to be beneficial to some individuals suffering from various medical conditions, some people may be advised against practicing certain styles, techniques and activities, such as free fighting or San Shou/San Da, on medical grounds. Students wishing to practice such activities may be asked to produce written consent from their doctor.

Clearly, as a teacher, it is important to treat all individuals with equal respect and try to ensure that everyone has equal access to your classes, as far as possible. An ethos of equality doesn't arise from a desire to be seen to be 'politically correct', it comes from a genuine acceptance of people just as they are and an awareness that, ultimately, whatever our perceived differences, we are all human.

Here are some definitions to think about. Some may be obvious, others less so.

Prejudice. This is pre-conceived, irrational judgment based on ignorance and assumed, rather than actual, characteristics. It is fuelled by stereotypes in society and is a type of mental rigidity that allows a person to maintain their existing preconceptions, regardless of any new information.

Stereotyping. This means having a fixed image and classifying all people in a particular group as if they are the same. Research has shown that these impressions can be formed on the basis of an encounter with only one individual thought to be representative of that group. This can prevent individuals from developing and displaying their full human potential.

Discrimination. This is actually defined as the ability to choose, consider and evaluate alternatives. It can be positive or negative, hidden (covert) or obvious (overt).

Positive discrimination. This is where preferential treatment is offered for the benefit of disadvantaged people, such as providing a fee-waiver for a student who you know to be struggling financially, or giving extra support to someone with a physical or learning disability.

Negative discrimination. This is behaviour arising from prejudice - favouring one group or individual over another - e.g. sexism, racism, ageism, fatism or use of words such as 'the handicapped'. An example might be selectively encouraging young, fit males to attend your martial arts class and discouraging anyone who is elderly, disabled, female or overweight on the assumption that it won't interest them or they won't be able to do it.

Overt discrimination. This includes taunts, snubs, sneers, jokes, abusive language or harassment, or speaking over people and ignoring their presence. While jokes may seem like harmless fun, they can contribute to a general culture in which put-downs of a certain group of people become tolerated and this can escalate to worse forms of discrimination.

Covert discrimination. This is hidden and subtle, e.g. not inviting someone who is gay to a party or interview or discouraging females, older people or overweight people from joining martial arts classes.

Individual discrimination. This is discrimination against individuals. Examples include: avoiding someone who is from a different ethnic background to yourself; not listening to a child or someone with a learning disability; or speaking only to the carer of a person in a wheelchair and ignoring their presence or talking about them as if they are unable to speak for themselves.

Institutional discrimination. This could include buildings with no access for disabled people or parents with small children, or 'Mother and Baby' rooms situated inside the ladies' lavatory so that fathers have nowhere to change their infants.

Questions to ask yourself

Although you may not have your own class yet, you can answer these with respect to classes where you assist with teaching or in your own future classes, once you are established.

- Do people really have equal access to your classes?

- Do you, either consciously or subconsciously, find yourself discouraging certain people from joining your classes? For example, if you live in an area with a diverse population and all your students are female and over fifty, you might ask why that is happening. Is it because you discourage anyone else from joining? Was the group set up as a community venture specifically for older people? Do any male students feel outnumbered and uncomfortable and so give up after a couple of sessions? If only females over fifty have ever applied, might that be because your website or publicity materials show only older females in your classes? Might it just be that media items on Tai Chi tend to focus on the benefits for older people and so younger people are not aware that it is suitable for them?

- When hiring premises for classes, do you consider problems of stairs, changing facilities or crèche provision? It might not be possible to provide ideal facilities when you are struggling to make a living and have little choice about where you teach, but if you eventually establish a large school, spread over a wide area, these points are worth bearing in mind.

- Can everyone see what you are doing and hear and understand what you are saying? An equal opportunity to learn means having access to a full learning experience, as far as is possible. Most difficulties can be overcome if the will is there. You might need to speak a little louder for someone with hearing difficulties, for example, or let them see your mouth so that they can lip-read, or turn the music down if it interferes with someone's hearing aid. One of our students was completely blind but, by listening and through occasional touch, he was able to learn the form better than the other twenty-five people in the class!

As well as considering your own thoughts and feelings, it's worth considering what you would do if you found your students behaving in a discriminatory manner towards each other.

- If you heard people in your class making racist, sexist or other discriminatory comments, even if they were joking, how would you deal with that?

Hopefully, by being aware, you can put a stop to it quickly by showing your disapproval. Keeping quiet can be misinterpreted as agreement or approval.

Sometimes, it might not be someone's words, but their behaviour that causes you concern. For example, a student who refuses to push hands with a person of different race, or someone who is using push hands as an opportunity to make unwelcome advances towards another student. In such cases, you are not only ethically responsible for making sure that your students have an enjoyable and non-discriminatory learning experience, you also have a duty of care to ensure their safety.

With the best will in the world, most people have prejudices of one kind or another. For example, someone with a strong local accent may feel uncomfortable speaking to 'posh' people. Someone who is trying to establish a reputation by training students to win martial arts competitions might feel frustrated that most of their students are older women who are only interested in the relaxation and health benefits. It is possible that these feelings, even if they are only subconscious, can result in some members of a class being neglected, particularly in a mixed ability class where you go from one person to another giving individual help.

It is useful, at the end of any lesson, to ask yourself:

- Did everyone have some input?
- If anyone was overlooked, why was that?
- Is this person frequently overlooked?
- If so, how does this happen? Are they just very quiet? Do they always stand at the back because they are shy or don't want to be noticed?
- Does this person somehow make you feel uneasy so that you tend to avoid them?

Just by being aware of any inequality in your teaching, you are more able to put that right in future classes.

Every person is different and you can't possibly be aware of all the ideas and expectations in the mind of every student who comes through your door, but you can make a habit of imagining how you would feel if that was you walking into someone else's class, and then do everything you can to make that person feel welcome.

Step 2

Teach Safely

By now, you may be looking forward to welcoming a diverse crowd of individuals through your doors and you are probably wondering when we are going to look at how to actually teach them some Tai Chi.

We will be getting to that very soon, but first we need to think carefully about how you can look after them when they get there so that they don't end up going out of your class feeling worse than when they came in!

Before you take on any students, you will need to have professional indemnity insurance, which we will discuss in Step 6, but preventing problems is always preferable to dealing with them.

The many benefits to health and well-being enjoyed by Tai Chi practitioners worldwide, according to scientific studies such as those carried out by the Harvard Medical School, are dependent on three things:

1. That what they are learning is actually Tai Chi. In other words, their teacher is practicing an authentic style of Tai Chi and this is being performed properly, following recognised Tai Chi principles. We will assume that you are indeed offering a recognised style of Tai Chi.

2. That Tai Chi is taught to them safely, by which we mean that they are learning to move in a way that does not cause them any kind of injury, such as damage to joints, during their Tai Chi forms and also during any warm-up exercises or martial training that accompanies them.

3. They are being taught in an environment that is as risk-free as possible. Risk assessments, whether formally recorded in writing, or a kind of general awareness that you maintain all the time, are part and parcel of teaching any subject, especially martial arts, so we will look at those in a moment.

Meanwhile let's get down to the bedrock of Tai Chi teaching: how to move safely.

How to Teach Warm-Ups Safely

Like most exercise classes, Tai Chi classes usually start with some warm-up exercises to loosen joints, stretch the muscles and boost the circulation before embarking on any other activities. There are endless possibilities and each teacher tends to have their own favourites.

Although, in a Tai Chi class, the warm-ups do not need to be particularly strenuous and may include gentle stretches and qigong, it is very important to think about what you are doing and why, since injury to students resulting from unsafe warm-up exercises could be a potential cause for litigation.

As a teacher of any kind of exercise, you need to have some idea of what the body is capable of and the risks that can arise from inappropriate exercise or from prolonged inactivity. In particular, you need to know the natural range of movement of joints.

To maintain full mobility, each joint should be taken through its full range of movement fairly regularly. This is particularly important for the shoulder joints, which can stiffen up when underused. The shoulders move very little during Tai Chi forms, since they are always kept down and level when the movements are done correctly, so the warm-ups at the start of the session provide a good opportunity to make up for this by gently circling the arms and shoulders a few times.

When you are new to teaching, a good way to remember the exercises you intend to do when you are actually standing out there in front of a class, is to either start at the top of the body and work downwards from the neck via the shoulders, wrists, hands and waist right down to the ankles and feet, or to start at the feet and work upwards.

Be very careful not to treat a hinge joint (such as a knee or elbow) as if it were a ball and socket joint (such as a shoulder or hip) during your warm up exercises. In the past British physiotherapists have expressed their concern about several movements that were once a common feature of exercise classes and were also a common source of injury. These are now listed by many organisations as 'contra-indicated', i.e. don't do them!

Here's why:

- Circling the knees can cause injuries to the knee joints.

- Circling the head, or any jerky neck movements, can cause dizziness and neck injuries.

- Touching the toes with straight legs from standing can cause back injuries and coming back up again with a straight back can increase the load on the spine by up to ten times!

- Sit ups with straight legs can cause back injuries.

- Lying on your back and raising both legs from the floor can cause back injuries or, for ladies, a prolapsed uterus. Most Tai Chi classes would not involve lying on the floor anyway but it is worth noting that lying flat can cause acid reflux if someone has a hiatus hernia and anyone with congestive heart failure could find it difficult to breathe in that position.

- Keeping the arms above the head for long periods can be very dangerous for people with heart problems as it puts a strain on the heart.

Judging the level

In general, when teaching warm-up or other kinds of exercise:

Teach the whole class according to the lowest common denominator in terms of physical fitness and ability.

If you aim for the middle or a majority of very fit and able students, you can advise everyone to 'only do what they know they can do comfortably' and some of them may follow this advice. However, others may push themselves beyond their limits in an attempt to keep up with everyone else and not lose face in front of the class; thereby running the risk of heart attack, stroke or injury.

Therefore, you need to be aware of the elderly gentleman in the back row with a heart condition or the lady with the hip replacement in the corner and make sure your exercises are safe for them, rather than focus on the majority. They can always do other exercises once the class has split into groups.

People who have had a hip replacement will be unable to do any movement which involves crossing one leg behind or in front of the other, such as Chen Style Wave Hands in Clouds, or Master Points the Way in the second Eighteen Tai Chi Qi Gong.

Anyone who has had a joint replacement is best advised to do smaller movements generally, listen to their own body and follow any instructions given to them by their physician.

Do resist any temptation to show off your own fitness and flexibility. You might think that this is obvious but we have seen it happen. As teachers, we all have to remember that our students are not there to be amazed by our abilities; we are there to help them to develop their own.

Why do we do warm-ups?

For an average beginners' Tai Chi class, where students are performing a very simple, slow sequence that is no more demanding than walking across a room, warm up exercises may not be strictly essential in the first place, though a lot of people enjoy doing Qigong exercises, such as the Eight Pieces of Brocade or Eighteen Tai Chi

Qigong, in the warm ups and for elderly people these may be easier than the actual form.

When students will be practicing more challenging activities, such as sequences involving kicks, or difficult movements like Snake Creeps Down, or weapons forms, push hands and martial applications, they will need a good warm up to boost their circulation and to warm and stretch their muscles.

The main purpose of the qigong warm up at the beginning of a class is to calm and clear the mind, release tension and help the student to relax, connect mind and body, and prepare to enjoy the forms. However, depending on which Qigong exercises you select, they can also provide a range of other benefits. For example, the Zhang Zhuang (or Zhang Zhong) posture is useful for helping to prevent arthritis, and for allowing people to learn to sink and root and to develop their 'peng jing' or ward-off energy. More dynamic qigong exercises may strengthen, loosen and stretch the body in various ways.

The difference between Qigong and Neigong

As you will know if you are an experienced Tai Chi student and you are planning to teach Tai Chi, qigong exercises or 'energy work' involve the transmission of energy along the meridians of the body and they usually involve a visualisation of this process as the exercises are performed. Less well known are the neigong exercises, which go further than the usual qigong exercises by assisting with the cultivation of internal power or inner strength. Neigong exercises are normally only practiced in classes that focus on training the martial aspects of Tai Chi Chuan and then only by very experienced students. They will normally involve:

- Loosening
- Relaxing
- Stretching
- Gathering
- Storing
- Releasing/applying

All of the above should be accompanied by appropriate dantien breathing, which we have described in detail in Volume 1 of this series: *How to Move Towards Tai Chi Mastery*, and again, in slightly less detail, in Volume 2: *How to Use Tai Chi for Self-defence*. The neigong exercises may also include auxiliary breath training for combat or meditation.

To stretch or not to stretch?

This has long been a hotly-debated subject in fitness circles. To the best of our knowledge, there is currently no evidence that stretching protects muscles from injury; in fact it has been shown to weaken subsequent performance where explosive energy is used. It does, however, increase the range of movement.

Recent research has shown that stretching muscles causes the production of resolvin, a substance that reduces inflammation, so it may well be beneficial.

Any stretching exercises should be done by slowly moving into position and holding the stretch and then slowly releasing, rather than using jerky or bouncy movements. Warm up the muscles first, perhaps by marching on the spot to stimulate overall circulation, before stretching them.

We may also take a particular movement of a form and practice it during the warm ups as preparation for its inclusion in the sequence later on.

Always advise students to listen to their own body and do only what they can do. If they find a particular movement too challenging due to specific problems, such as a frozen shoulder, stiff knees or an old ankle injury, work with them to find a safe alternative that is comfortable for them.

How to Teach Tai Chi Forms Safely

The most likely sources of potential injury when learning Tai Chi forms are:

- failure to turn in the back foot to a comfortable angle when changing direction, resulting in twisting of the ankle, the hip and especially the knee;

- failure to turn the waist before turning out a front foot when moving forwards, again putting a strain on the leg joints and allowing weight to be shifted into a twisted leg;

- leaning forward and over-extending the arms in push positions, putting a strain on the back;

- locking out the back knee and over-bending the front knee in forward stances so that the knee goes beyond the toes, thereby putting excessive strain on the front knee joint and the lower back;

- spinning on one foot with full body weight on it in moves such as turn to kick with left heel or turn and sweep lotus, thereby risking ankle or knee injuries (particularly risky of the student is performing the movement on carpeted flooring or while wearing rubber-soled trainers that stick to the floor), rather than taking the turn in comfortable, balanced stages;

- repetitive strain injuries from practicing movements over and over, especially difficult ones such as Snake Creeps Down or kicks; or easier movements where the weight is all on one leg, such as White Crane Spreads Wings or Play Guitar/Lute/Pippa; or prolonged push hands;

- kicking too high without adequate preparation;

- kicking during pregnancy (the ligaments supporting the hip joints relax during the third trimester and can be strained by over-use, making it more difficult to regain full mobility following the birth);

- incorrect practice of fa jin (fa jing or fajin).

How to Teach Fa Jin Safely

Remember, in fa jin, you need to encourage students to:

- Protect the head from undue vibration, by correct structure, stability, sinking and rooting, so that shock waves travel outwards rather than upwards into the head.
- Protect the pelvic floor by gently squeezing the pelvic floor muscles (closing the chi gates) and directing the lower abdominal force forwards and upwards (rolling the dantien) rather than straight down.
- Protect the umbilicus by breathing correctly (reverse breathing), rolling the dantien and pulling in the midriff, avoiding pushing out the whole abdomen.
- Protect the nasal cavity by opening the mouth and breathing 'Hwa' as they exhale.
- Only practice it occasionally. Don't overdo it and risk injury from overuse.

There is a detailed explanation of Tai Chi breathing in our book: *How to Move Towards Tai Chi Mastery*.

You need to be able to do it safely yourself before attempting to teach it to others, so check with your instructor if you are unsure.

How to Teach Martial Skills Safely

If you want to teach any kind of partner work, such as martial applications and push hands, you need to:

1. provide a safe and suitable environment,
2. arrange adequate insurance cover for yourself and your students,
3. provide careful instruction in these skills, and
4. ensure adequate supervision throughout each session.

We will look in detail at how to go about the practicalities of teaching martial applications and push hands in Step 3 and we will offer our advice on how to get insurance in Step 6. For now, let's look at what we mean by a safe environment for general teaching purposes and especially for teaching the martial skills of Tai Chi.

Providing a Safe Environment

In the UK, the Health and Safety at Work Act makes it the responsibility of every employer to make their workplace as safe as possible, warn all employees of any dangers, provide training in safe work practices, provide protective clothing or equipment if needed and take any complaints or suggestions seriously. They should also provide adequate first aid cover. It also states that the employee is responsible for following the guidance given by their employer and reporting unsafe practices.

Although we are talking here about your students and not your employees, the above policy is a useful guide and you should do your utmost to protect their health and safety. You are advised to carry out a risk assessment on any teaching premises you use and your students need to be aware of any risks and follow any guidance you give them relating to health and safety.

You may also be an employee yourself, perhaps working as a part time tutor for a local college, and will therefore need to work in accordance with any laws and the organisation's Health and Safety policy.

It is important to be aware of health and safety issues at all times. If there is any risk to any person from what you or they are doing, or there are problems with the environment in which you are teaching, what you have is an accident waiting to happen and it's not a good idea to put it out of your mind and hope that the fact that it hasn't happened yet will mean it is unlikely to happen in the future. For example:

- If you are teaching in a studio with floor to ceiling mirrors on the walls, never allow students to push hands or practice martial applications in a place where it is possible that one of them could be pushed into a mirror. The same applies to windows.

- If students are using weapons, make sure that they have sufficient space to practice without hitting each other and that their weapons are in good condition. A whirling broadsword which falls to bits mid-whirl can do a lot of damage.

- If you demonstrate applications on a student, never use undue force, and make sure they know what to expect. Don't throw them onto the floor unless they know how to fall and there are appropriate mats for them to fall onto.

- If there is a problem with ventilation, heating or cooling in the premises you are using, report it to an appropriate person.

- If equipment is stored at the side of the room, make sure this is stacked safely and not likely to trip up, or fall onto, your students.

- Also report any other hazards such as frayed carpets, uneven flooring, slippery surfaces, sharp protrusions or electrical faults. Don't ever feel that you are being a nuisance by raising your concerns with managers. Having you tell them several times about poor lighting and the little hole in the car park tarmac is preferable to an expensive court case when someone breaks an ankle by stepping into it in the dark.

- If you are teaching full combat martial arts, make sure you have adequate mats to cover the whole floor space you are using and that these are in good condition, thick enough to absorb a fall and fitted together properly so they don't slip around. Gaps can cause trips, twisted ankles or a hard surface to fall onto.

- Punch bags, kick bags and any other training equipment should also be checked regularly.

Risk Assessments

Some employers or managers of hired premises will require you to complete a formal risk assessment of your teaching area. This is usually just a form on which you report any concerns you might have as you walk through the premises with the safety of your students in mind.

If the form you are given is unsuitable for the type of class you are teaching, discuss this with your employer and maybe offer to design a better one, which may be gratefully received as long as it is clear, easy to use and contains all the necessary information. The strangest one we came across was about fifteen pages long and was designed for building contractors and electricians. When whittled down to what was relevant, this became a single sheet of A4! Fortunately, our employers found this acceptable and we were relieved to find that we were not actually responsible for the safe wiring of the premises!

Whether or not you need to write down any concerns, it is advisable to do so. At the very least, you can report them verbally to whoever is in charge and make the area as safe as possible.

Your Own Health and Safety Policy

Having your own Health and Safety policy is good professional practice. It could be something quite simple, like this:

While Tai Chi can be a very gentle form of exercise, it is also a martial art; therefore reasonable care must be taken when practicing martial applications or training with weapons.

Students wishing to practice push hands and martial applications, or to use weapons, need to be licenced to practice martial arts and have member-to-member insurance.

Students should be suitably dressed in loose-fitting clothing and appropriate footwear.

Students suffering from certain medical conditions may be advised against certain activities, such as free fighting, unless they have written approval from their doctor.

Share this with your students. If there is an incident in which legal action is threatened, it can be helpful to have evidence that the student was aware of these basic requirements.

For example, consider the following situation:

You have advised a student about appropriate footwear but the student comes to class in shoes with a narrow heel and does a spinning kick which damages the floor and results in the student losing her balance and wrenching her ankle. Both she and the owner of the premises threaten to sue you.

- Who is responsible for this situation?
- How might the situation have been avoided?
- What evidence might there be that might help to disprove your negligence?

We know of one instance, many years ago, where a lady deliberately went around all the classes in her area begging instructors to push her a little so that she could 'feel their chi'! On the slightest touch, she would fall over, pretend to hurt her ankle and go straight to a solicitor. Fortunately, the fact that she made a habit of this meant that her scam was quickly discovered, but not before she had caused considerable distress to several good teachers.

This case, however, made everyone more aware of the need for insurance for themselves and their students. If you ever have an incident in your class that causes you concern, write down everything that happened and ask any witnesses to do the same. Be aware that such situations are possible and do what you can to avoid them by ensuring that everyone knows the safety requirements in your class and never rise to the challenge of demonstrating your fa jin on someone, particularly a newcomer.

In a court of law, you would be held accountable if you knowingly put the safety of your students or others at risk or if your negligence resulted in injury to people or damage to property. Negligence could include allowing students to harm each other due to inadequate instruction or supervision.

Incidents involving student misconduct

Misconduct can range from minor 'messing about' to an act of premeditated violence resulting in criminal prosecution. In between, there are a host of possibilities which may necessitate anything from a friendly verbal warning to exclusion from your school, or even criminal proceedings.

Since most Tai Chi students are likely to be adults, such incidents will normally be few and far between, but it is worth considering different ways of handling them or, better still, avoiding them. Some martial arts schools have a Code of Conduct on the wall or inside a membership card and a system of verbal warnings, written warnings or exclusion, depending on the circumstances.

However, take care not to overdo the warning thing. Adults can find it patronising and children can find it very off-putting, as it implies a lack of trust. We tend to find expectations of mature and sensible behaviour preferable to threats.

Questions to ask yourself

- What are the specific hazards in the place(s) where you teach (or assist with teaching)?

- How could you ensure that any risks are kept to a minimum?

- In all the premises you use, where are the fire exits?

- In all the premises you use, where is the first aid box kept, and is it well stocked?

- In all the premises you use, where is the accident book kept?

- In all the premises you use, is there a named first aider on duty at all times, or is that you?

- Imagine that a couple of teenagers have recently joined your class. Their member-to-member insurance is not yet through and you have taught them the first movements of a form and left them to practice. Half way through the lesson you see them sparring with each other in a corner of the room. How would you deal with this situation?

- During a pushing hands session, two of your students are getting a bit carried away. They are both using excessive external force and you can see from their faces that they are no longer doing this as a learning exercise but are out to injure one another. What would you do?

Dealing with Emergencies

Even in the safest possible environment and with the best teaching in the world, students may occasionally feel unwell or be injured accidentally during a class. You need to know what to look out for if they are unwell and what to do if they need medical attention.

Warning signs to look out for

Although Tai Chi is normally no more strenuous than walking slowly around a room, in advanced classes, some parts of the training and practice can be very demanding, particularly prolonged pushing hands sessions and free-fighting.

Signs of discomfort

Breathlessness, palpitations, red or purple skin, excessive sweating, pain and discomfort are not desirable effects of exercise, particularly in older people. These may be warning signs that the person is overdoing it and needs to rest.

Signs of distress

People with heart conditions, high blood pressure or lung conditions need to be particularly careful when exercising. Flushed red skin, pallor, greyness or blueness around the mouth and nose, or inside the lips, are signs that the person may be in distress and in need of urgent medical attention.

Ideally, exercise teachers and martial arts instructors should be trained in first aid and resuscitation techniques and, if possible, have a current first aid certificate.

While it is easy to see that overdoing any kind of exercise can be hazardous to health, it might be more surprising to discover that people sometimes faint in a gentle Tai Chi class due to a fall in blood pressure because it is so very relaxing. This is particularly likely if the person is taking medication to lower blood pressure but has made lifestyle choices that lower it naturally as well. One of our students once wore a continuous heart monitor for several days. Her physician noticed a marked dip in blood pressure which then gradually returned to the previous level. This coincided with her Tai Chi class and lasted for several hours after the class. While this is a very positive effect, people taking medications should be aware that it exists.

First aid training

Not all employers will insist that you have first aid training, though some might. Either way, it is a good idea to attend an approved First Aid training course every few years so that you would know what to do if a student had an accident or medical incident while in your class.

At the very least, you should read a good, current First Aid Manual, such as the one written by the St John Ambulance Brigade and the British Red Cross, so that you can answer the following questions.

Questions to ask yourself

What would you do if a student in your class:

- had chest pains (possible angina or heart attack)?
- had a stroke?
- had an asthma attack?
- had an epileptic seizure?
- was diabetic and looked very unwell or confused in your class?
- cut themselves badly on glass from a broken mirror?
- scalded themselves while making a cup of tea?
- lost consciousness?

What to do in an emergency

Recent research has shown that, in an extreme emergency, most people tend to freeze rather than escape, unless they know in advance what to do. So, in any premises where you teach, you and your students all need to know what to do if there is a fire, bomb alert or other emergency situation. This will include, for example, knowing where the fire exits are and where to assemble outside the building until help arrives. In some places, it may include knowing where there is a safe place to hide if a different type of incident, such as a gun crime, is taking place.

In general, if there is a fire:

1. Get everyone out.

2. Get the firefighters out.

3. Stay out until you are told it's safe to go back in.

If you can, take your register with you so that you can check that all your students are out of the building, but don't go back in to get it..

If a student is injured or becomes unwell during your class:

1. Make the area safe for yourself, the injured person and any bystanders. An injured first-aider is not much use to the casualty. For example, don't kneel on broken glass while helping a student who cut themselves by falling into a wall mirror or window.

2. Provide support to anyone who is injured by:

- calling for help (or get someone else to do that but, if so, check that they have done it and help is on its way);

- giving First Aid.

3. Afterwards:

- Gather witness testimonies from anyone who saw what happened.
- Complete any relevant accident reports or incident reports.
- If you are working for someone else at the time, report it to your line manager.

OK, so now that you have provided your students with a safe and welcoming learning environment, you have some idea of why they are there, you know what bits of information might need to be written down and you know what to do in an emergency, we can finally begin to explore how best to go about communicating your hard-earned Tai Chi skills and knowledge to them and ensuring that they have the most effective and enjoyable learning experience you can possibly provide. Hopefully, this will also mean that you will have the most enjoyable teaching experience too!

Step 3

Communicate

Now it's time to get to the business of how you can best communicate your knowledge and skills to other people. We'll begin with a look at general principles of good communication and go on to explore a range of ways to pass on your practical skills and knowledge of Tai Chi.

Potential Barriers to Learning

One of the most valuable skills for any teacher is an ability to put complex ideas into simple terms so that other people can understand them clearly. Even when an idea is very clear in your own mind and you do your absolute best to transfer that same idea to the mind of another person, there's no guarantee that the idea they end up with is anything like the one you intended. There might be many reasons for this.

Problems with sending your message

- Maybe you didn't express it as clearly as you thought you did.
- Maybe your voice was too quiet or you mumbled a bit.
- Maybe you were speaking too fast or deluging them with too much information so that they had no chance to take it all in.

- Maybe you used jargon or words that the other person was not familiar with.

- Maybe you were turned away from them so that they couldn't hear you, read your lips or see what you were showing them.

Problems with the environment

- Maybe noise from the central heating, air conditioning or ventilation system or the volume of the background music prevented half the class from hearing you.

- Maybe the people at the back couldn't see you or there were other people in the way.

- Maybe the room was too cold or too hot and they were too uncomfortable to give you their full attention.

Problems with receiving your message

- Maybe the student had reduced hearing or vision, or perhaps a learning disability.

- Perhaps the student did not speak your language or was unfamiliar with your local dialect.

- Maybe they really couldn't do what you just described and demonstrated because of physical or medical difficulties.

- Maybe they had some existing knowledge or belief that caused them to disagree with what you were saying and they 'switched off' from that point.

- Maybe they didn't want to do that movement whose martial application you just explained because the thought made them very uncomfortable for ethical reasons.

- Maybe they didn't want to do partner work because it meant allowing someone into their personal space, perhaps as a result of unpleasant experiences in the past.

Overcoming barriers

There's a lot you can do to overcome most of these challenges. Here are a few suggestions to bear in mind:

- Be aware of background noise and keep it to a minimum, if possible.

- Speak loudly and clearly enough to allow all your students to hear you, without shouting. Check this out with the students at the back of the room and be aware of anyone who has already told you that they have hearing difficulties.

- Encourage new starters or people with any visual or hearing impairment to stand near the front. It's ironic that new learners, who have the greatest need to see what is going on, are also the ones most likely to try to 'hide' on the back row so they don't embarrass themselves by letting experienced students see them 'doing it wrong'. You can provide encouragement but if they are very resistant to coming forwards, don't try to force the issue and so put them off coming back.

- Keep the jargon to a minimum, particularly with beginners. Like most disciplines, Tai Chi has its own jargon words that mean nothing to a beginner. Words like 'sinking', 'rooting', 'softness' and 'energy' are quite tricky concepts to grasp, so they need to be explained carefully and must eventually be experienced by students before any real understanding can be achieved.

- A further problem in Tai Chi is that many Chinese terms are also used. It is easy to forget that some people in the class may never have heard of 'song' and 'chi' and 'peng jing/jin'. Even for those who have, it may take years to reach a good level of understanding of such concepts. Teachers who liberally pepper every sentence with such words, irrespective of their listener's level of experience and comprehension, can leave their students in a perpetual fog, leading to frustration and de-motivation.

- Some (non-Chinese) teachers use lots of Chinese words in their classes, possibly in the belief that having a Chinese word for everything makes them sound more knowledgeable and authentic. In reality there is nothing particularly inspiring about a person who seems completely incapable of calling a sword a sword; they are just creating another unnecessary barrier to learning.

- The next essential is to be sure of your facts, or as sure as you can be. There's no point spending time and energy putting information across if the information is wrong. Obviously, everyone makes mistakes and none of us know everything. There will inevitably be times when you have to apologise for a bit of misinformation you have inadvertently passed on. Professional integrity lies in teaching to the best of your knowledge and continuing to develop your own skills and understanding for the benefit of your students. Your honesty will be appreciated, while a glossed-over mistake may be assumed to be a fact and so be carried forward into the next generation.

- It is also important to be clear about which parts of your teaching are widely accepted as true and which are based on your own personal opinion. If you don't know the answer to a question, it's best to admit it and promise that you will try to find out, rather than make up some impressive-sounding waffle. Temporary embarrassment at not being an all-knowing guru is better than the complete loss of credibility that can result from the discovery that you have not been honest with your students.

- Be prepared to modify your approach to meet the specific needs of your students. It sounds obvious but it's important to remember that you are there for them, not the other way around. If you really have their best interests at heart, you will avoid becoming too dogmatic in your approach. Never let yourself think you know everything and that you have to drum it into every person who comes through your door. Avoid jumping ahead too quickly and leaving them in a fog. Start where they are now and help them to build on that.

- Listen to your students. You may end up learning as much from them as they learn from you. Teaching is a dynamic,

> two-way process of exploration and discovery. It's a bit like taking friends on a mountain trail that's new to them but that you know well. As you point out familiar sights, they might draw your attention to things you hadn't noticed before because they are looking with fresh eyes. That's where the real joy comes from – that and helping them to reach the summit without getting lost among the side tracks or falling off a cliff!

In the rest of this section, we will look at tried and tested methods for passing on your Tai Chi skills and knowledge.

Passing on Your Tai Chi Skills

Some of the following practical considerations may seem simple and obvious but they can make a big difference to the effectiveness of your teaching of Tai Chi forms.

Where do I stand?

There are various opinions about where the teacher should stand when teaching a Tai Chi sequence to a class. Let's consider the pros and cons of some of the options.

We once read a review of a video of ours, written by a very disgruntled customer who complained that it "showed a man doing Tai Chi"! Worse still, she said, he did it facing towards her, which was confusing because he was going the wrong way, and then he did it facing away from her, which meant that she couldn't see his arms. This neatly sums up the perennial problem with teaching Tai Chi forms.

Students occasionally ask us to face them so that they can see what our hands are doing and we have duly obliged. For this to work at all, we have to do it going in the opposite direction so that they can mirror us. Invariably, everyone is fine during the opening movements, while we are facing them, but as soon as there is a ninety degree turn to the side, the whole thing breaks down because students forget they are supposed to be mirroring and start copying exactly and thereby start to use the wrong arm.

So most of the time, we face away from our students so that everyone is going in the same direction and we are all using the correct limbs for each manoeuvre. We might occasionally turn around to show them a particular movement from the front and then assume the facing away position again.

As you have probably discovered for yourself when you were learning Tai Chi, the best place for a student to stand is a little behind and a little to the side of the teacher; occasionally swapping sides so that they can see from a different angle.

Mirrors on the wall

It can help to have mirrors along one wall so that students can then copy the teacher from behind and occasionally glance in the mirror to check the bits that they can't see. However, there are two potential pitfalls where mirrors are concerned:

1. Some students only look at the reflected image and end up making mistakes because a) it is harder to copy the movements from a reflected image and b) the depth

perception is not very good in the mirror, so it is actually better to look directly at the instructor.

2. When practicing on their own, some students become mesmerised by their own reflection, so that their head becomes glued in a forward facing position and they either forget to turn their waist at all or turn it from side to side without allowing their head to go with it. If this happens, it can be useful for them to do the form facing the other way sometimes or to do it with their eyes closed so that they start to feel the internal connectedness instead of being externally focused on what it looks like.

Glued to the spot

Whether or not you have mirrors in any particular class, we recommend that you encourage your students to move around as much as possible and get a different view from time to time. In every class, we generally find that each student tends to pick a place in the room to stand and then gets quite attached to it. Some like to always hide at the back; others might always want to be directly behind the teacher, or have a favourite spot at the left or right side of the room. So every time the whole class performs the sequence, they have the same view and may miss something important that one arm or leg is doing, just because their view of it is always obscured. For this reason, we sometimes invite students to swap places with someone on the opposite side of the room or ask the back row to come to the front.

If you are teaching a student one-to-one, this is not usually a problem, as you can both continually adjust your position so that they get to see every movement clearly. In a large class, however, it can be a problem, especially when people at the back refuse to come further forward and their view is always obstructed by other students.

Deploy your troops!

If you have any experienced students in the class, it is useful to ask them to take up positions around the edge of the group so that, whichever way the rest of the students are facing in any part of the form, if they can't see you they can always see someone who knows what they are doing. This presupposes that you are all going at the same speed and your movements are well synchronised, otherwise they will end up even more confused!

How far do I go?

When you are teaching a form to new learners, you may ask yourself if it is best to:

1. Teach several movements roughly and then go back and correct them later, or

2. Teach just one or two moves and make sure the student is doing them properly before going on to the next one.

From many years of experience, we can say that the second alternative is usually best. It is at least twice as difficult to undo bad habits as it is to learn something from scratch. Teaching too much too quickly is the most common mistake that trainee Tai Chi teachers make.

We can recall many occasions in the past where we have asked someone to take a newcomer through the first couple of movements of the form and turned around five minutes later to see that they are half-way through the sequence. The assistant instructor is very pleased to have taken them so far, while the poor student, of course, is very confused and can't remember any of it.

This is very understandable. Someone who is new to teaching may be feeling nervous and be worried about whether or not they will be able to remember the movements under pressure. It may also seem natural to assume that the new student will copy your moves exactly, and remember everything you show them or tell them.

However, just because you have shown them a particular move a few times and asked them if they have got it, and they nod, that doesn't mean they have actually got it. The only way to find out is by watching them do it by themselves and checking the important points, especially their posture and footwork to ensure their safety, before moving on to the next movement.

Occasionally, there will be students who feel the need to rocket through the form any old way, perhaps from a competitive streak, or a desire to 'catch up with everyone else' or from boredom or demotivation caused by going through the same few moves many times without 'getting it'. You will need to use your own professional judgment in each individual case. Perhaps sometimes, for the sake of someone's self-esteem or maintaining their interest, you might need to sacrifice accuracy in order to allow students to get the overall mental map of the form and then go back to perfect it.

However, do bear in mind that some will never bother to go back and improve it at all and then insist that their own interpretation is the way you taught them! Some may even go out and set up a class of their own after a few lessons! It is worth remembering that your students are your 'shop window' and people will judge you on the abilities of your former students when they show the world what they have learned from you.

Comings and goings

There are some types of class where it is almost impossible to teach everyone the form correctly due to the weekly appearance of new starters with no previous experience of Tai Chi. If you have experienced students who are willing to act as assistant instructors in your class, or if you know that everyone is happy for you to go from group to group while they spend some time practicing on their own, this is not usually a problem; in fact it is the norm for most martial arts classes.

However, it can be difficult in a health club where, because they may have paid hefty membership fees, everyone may feel entitled to your undivided attention all the time. Perhaps the best you can do in such circumstances is to go over a couple of moves in detail with the whole class each week so that newcomers learn how at least some of it is done properly and safely while experienced students can 'polish' those movements and deepen their understanding of the Tai Chi principles. Over the weeks, everyone can then feel comfortable with more and more movements from the sequence when they go through the whole thing together at the end of the session.

The question then would be: which one or two movements should you teach during a particular session? It may be that you are working through the sequence in order, week by week, and new starters join in at whatever movement you are up to. Or perhaps you have had a major insight into the applications of cloud hands and are eager to share it with your class that day.

One approach we have found useful is to do a 'diagnostic' at the beginning of the session: allowing the whole class to do as much of the sequence as they currently know (while new starters watch to see what they are going to be learning) and then picking up on any particular moves they were finding difficulty with as your main focus for detailed tuition.

Obviously, what you teach is up to you. After a while, you will develop an instinct for what your students need to learn next and any small section of a form is an opportunity to explore the principles, which will be helpful to everyone, whatever their level of experience.

So, now that you have thought about where to stand and how much to teach, the next thing to decide is how to get your message across. Your choice will depend on your students, the subject you are trying to communicate, and your own strengths and preferences.

The EDIP method

A tried and tested way to pass on your practical skills is via the EDIP method:

1. **Explain** - Tell your students what you are about to do and why it's important.

2. **Demonstrate** - Show the students the skill they are about to learn.

3. **Imitate** - Let them copy what you are doing as you do it.

4. **Practice** - Give them time to practice, with and without you watching them and providing feedback.

Practicing the skills should make up more than half of the learning experience.

Remember the old saying: *'What I hear, I forget; what I see, I remember; what I do, I understand.'*

Some students are quite resistant to this idea. They want someone they can 'follow' and even ask you to 'talk them through it' every time. This is fine if they are only attending for a bit of enjoyment or if they have memory difficulties and really can't even begin to do it on their own, and if you don't mind having almost permanent laryngitis from non-stop talking in every class you teach. One of us did this for years until a student admitted: "Oh we don't listen to what you're saying, we just like the sound of your voice!"

It's worth remembering that you can entertain a class on a regular basis and risk leaving them with nothing if the class closes, or you can give them the confidence to do it on their own so that you leave them with a gift that can last a lifetime. We know of a couple who spent their life savings learning Tai Chi in China for two years and then came back to set up their own class, only to find that they couldn't remember the forms because they had never done them on their own!

Giving Feedback

By allowing your students time to practice on their own, you also give yourself time to look at what they are doing. When you are at the front of the class and practicing a form with them, they are behind you most of the time, so you can't see them, and you might assume that they are copying you exactly, which is actually highly unlikely.

When you do have a look at what your students are doing, give them positive feedback on what they did well. If they need to make any corrections, add them on the end of their achievements with the word "and" rather than "but". The word "and" continues a positive statement, whereas "but" can focus their attention on a negative that makes them feel as if they have failed in some way.

This process of observing, assessing and giving constructive feedback is known as 'formative assessment' and we will say more about it in the next chapter. It's what's missing when people try to learn Tai Chi from a video, with no teacher available to correct any mistakes. Combined with the EDIP method, it is probably the best method there is for communicating your practical skills to others effectively.

Peer support

Another reason never to feel guilty about asking students to practice on their own is that this is often the time when they actually have an opportunity to talk to each other and get to know each other. They can also help each other to learn. This is obvious when experienced students help newcomers but even when all the students are relative beginners, you can let them spend a few minutes practicing a few moves as a 'self-help group', helping each other if they get stuck.

Usually, different people struggle with different bits but between them they can get the whole thing. If someone has been struggling, they may be reassured to discover that others are struggling too.

If there is something that none of them quite understand, they may have the courage, collectively, to tell you so and this is brilliant feedback for you so you can go over it again and make a note to show and explain that part more carefully next time.

Sometimes, each group might want to elect a spokesperson to feed back their experiences to the whole class, thereby helping everyone to gain new insights.

All of this becomes easier as the students become more experienced and get to know each other well but our advice is to start this process as early as possible. If it is always seen as being a normal occurrence in classes, it will be less daunting than attempting to introduce it after months or years of having you personally leading the whole class all the time.

Here's a tip – if you ever cover a class for someone, find out what forms they are working on and also what teaching methods they use! If you take over a group that has been led by their instructor for years and you ask them to do their form on their own, you might find that half of them walk out or don't come back the following week!

Keep physical contact to a minimum

It is not normally necessary to touch a student when teaching them Tai Chi, unless:

- You are teaching them pushing hands or martial applications.

- A partially-sighted or blind student has asked you to place their limbs in the correct position or to feel your arm as it moves.

- People are struggling to learn a particular posture and you ask the whole class to hold the pose for a couple of minutes while you go around the room, gently moving an arm into the correct place, with their permission.

Make sure it is OK with each person and be particularly careful if the person is of a different gender to yourself. Religious beliefs can also make it unacceptable for some people to let you touch them and anyone dealing with past trauma could be very uncomfortable with the idea of having anyone too close to them.

If in doubt, don't touch them, just explain what they need to do, show them how to do it correctly, many times if you need to, and then let them find their own way, even if they get it wrong, unless they are risking their safety by doing it their way.

How to unstick stuckness

However good a teacher you are, it is inevitable that some students will pick up Tai Chi more quickly than others and some will continue to make the same mistakes over and over again, no matter how many times you explain or show them the correct way to do it. You need to have endless patience to help people to progress when they are stuck in this way.

One way that we have found helpful is to play the game of 'spot the deliberate mistake'. Ask your students to watch you carefully while you do the movement twice yourself, first your way and then their way, and ask them which is correct. Most students will be able to identify what they were doing wrongly and correct it then and there, but others may not see a difference or they may think that they were doing it your way all along.

People are complex and no two are exactly alike. There will be natural variations between the ease with which people are able to copy and remember your movements. If anyone is struggling, that doesn't always mean that they have not been watching or listening closely; it could be that their brain and body are giving them mixed messages about what they are seeing, hearing and doing.

For example, there is a large part of the brain, called the cerebellum, which is involved in translating the idea of how we want to move into the actual movements we make and then looking at the position we are in and comparing it with the one we intended. For some people, this area of the brain doesn't work very well so they may think that their hand is at shoulder-height when it is actually somewhere above their ear.

Other parts of the brain are also involved in the smooth coordination of movements and there can be a wide range of variation in the development of these regions, or in the degree to which communication is able to take place between the left and right hemispheres of the brain, so that some students may suffer from a condition called dyspraxia, which can affect them to varying degrees. Very mild cases may not have been previously diagnosed but could still affect their ability to learn the complex movements of Tai Chi.

These difficulties, which are surprisingly common, have nothing to do with a person's level of intelligence or ability to understand your instructions. We have had university lecturers and even qualified physiotherapists who have been unable to copy even the simplest postures without extreme difficulty. We have also had people with diagnosed 'learning difficulties' who have not had any problems with those movements.

Our advice would be to persevere, however long it takes. This is where your patience, imagination and creativity are tested to the maximum but, in many cases, you will be rewarded when they finally 'get it'. The satisfaction of that breakthrough tends to outweigh all the successes you had with their many classmates who picked it up straight away. However, you may just have to accept that some people may not get it even after twenty years of study. However frustrating this may be for you as a teacher, you can at least be happy to know that they are still enjoying coming to class and doing it their own way.

Passing on Your Knowledge

When it comes to sharing knowledge, don't overdo it. Most students are there to do rather than to listen and will be completely turned off by a half-hour 'info-dump', without any interaction, which evidences your brilliance on the subject but bores them to tears.

Talks and discussions

Occasionally, you may decide that you have a message that would best be conveyed by giving a short talk to the whole class, or you may decide that a group discussion would be better.

The ability to speak to your whole class is obviously an important skill but it can be quite a daunting prospect for someone new to teaching. Keeping your message brief, clear and simple can help you to keep focused and not lose track of what you are saying due to 'nerves'. If you are very good at public speaking you may be able to keep students riveted for a whole lesson, but most people have a fairly short concentration span and get bored after a while and, in martial arts classes, the main focus is normally on doing rather than listening, so short talks lasting no more than a few minutes are usually preferable to long lectures.

A group discussion allows students to be more interactive and express their opinions, and it also allows you to gain a better idea of whether they have understood what you are trying to say to them. It may be that you occasionally carry out a planned group discussion with the whole class on a particular subject, perhaps during a tea break, while at other times discussions arise naturally in a small group situation in response to a question from a student or a point in the teaching of a skill or principle.

You may discuss the point informally with the individual who asked the question, or with the small group with whom they were working, or you may feel that it is an important point that would benefit the whole class and therefore invite everyone to join in. Depending on the length and nature of the discussion, you may decide to remain standing or get everyone to sit down.

Older students, especially, may find sitting down for a few minutes a welcome relief as well as a chance to hear something interesting.

Large discussion groups take quite a bit of skill to handle well, in order to ensure that:

- everyone gets a fair chance to voice their opinion, if they wish to;
- misconceptions are clearly but tactfully dealt with, without making any member of the group feel foolish or embarrassed;
- the whole thing doesn't degenerate into everyone speaking at once or holding little sub-discussions within the group.

Some of the best discussions arise when you 'throw something into the pot' and let the students find their own solutions and understanding, with you acting as a guide and facilitator of the process.

If the discussion is about some practical point or one of the Tai Chi principles, then showing is usually better than telling and an opportunity to put the new knowledge into practice during or after the talk or discussion can be invaluable.

Handouts and websites

If you are not comfortable with speaking to large groups, you may feel happier with communicating some of your ideas in writing, perhaps as a handout for your students.

These will need to be clear, accurate and informative. If you have problems with writing but know what you want to say, you may find it easier to record and then transcribe it, or use voice-to-text software.

If your spelling is the problem, you could run it through a spell checker on a word processor or ask someone to read it and correct it before you do the final copy. As well as getting your message across, the quality of any handouts you produce affects other people's perception of your professional competence. It doesn't look good if you can't spell the name of your own martial art and offer them a handout on "Thai Chi" or "Tae Chi", for example.

However good your handouts are, you will probably find that some students value them, read them and keep them safe, while others may throw them in the bin on the way out. When you know your students well, you may say something like: "I have some handouts here; you can come and collect one on the way out if you are interested", thus saving trees. Putting them on a website also saves trees but not all students have computers, in which case handouts are useful as a back-up.

You may also recommend books and videos for your students to buy. Loaning them out to students can be quite expensive if they leave and don't return them. You may even decide to make your own videos or write your own books. Some teachers manage to supplement their incomes in this way, though the profits are normally very modest since the recording equipment, editing software, media, printing and online selling are surprisingly expensive and it is easy to inadvertently end up selling them for less than they cost you to make them.

Selling from your website will depend on how many people use that website. You can have a great shop but it won't sell much if nobody knows it's there. Selling on Amazon gets you a larger audience, but there are fees involved so any profits you make may still be minimal. Even so, it is good to know that you have provided something of value to a large number of people, even if you never get rich in the process and, for us anyway, that's what teaching Tai Chi is all about.

Some of the best books and videos are produced by people who have a real desire to share their knowledge and skills with others. Some of the worst are those produced by people who are just out to make lots of money. The quality of the production does not always correspond directly to the quality of the content. A cheap home video produced in the back garden of someone who really understands Tai Chi can be far more valuable to a student than a glitzy and expensive package with dubious content.

The challenge of finding ways to communicate Tai Chi to others can be one of the great joys of teaching. It can be frustrating at times but there are few moments in life more fulfilling for a teacher than when the eyes of a student light up, or they move in a certain way, and you know that they have finally 'got it'!

Teaching Push Hands and Martial Applications

The EDIP method works well when you are teaching the martial aspects of Tai Chi. As with teaching forms, there is a lot to explain and demonstrate first. Copying what you are doing is helpful as they begin to work with a partner. Most importantly, long hours of practice with various partners are absolutely essential if your students really want to learn and understand these skills.

On a one-to-one basis, there will be just yourself and the student doing the partner work together but if you are teaching a group, you will need to:

- Choose an experienced student or a willing volunteer to demonstrate the technique with.

- Let the students pair up and practice while you go round the class, offering help where needed. If any interesting questions or problems crop up, you can call a time out, bring the class together and go over that topic with everyone.

- If possible, push hands briefly with each person in the class so that you can feel, first hand, how they are getting on and offer them advice and correction. This is preferable to just watching them push hands with each other. The disadvantage is that you take your eyes off the rest of the class while you are engaged with one student, so it is more difficult to supervise what is going on in the rest of the room. For this reason, it is often best to practice push hands on those occasions when you have an even number of students present so that you are free to walk around.

Then again, if your students know and understand the ground rules, you can usually trust them to practice safely. If you also encourage them to keep the noise level generally low, you can maintain an overall awareness of the class as a whole, even while working with one student at a time. Ideally, you can pair up experienced students with less experienced students so that they can be learning from each other while you just provide overall supervision and help where needed.

Obviously, all push hands and applications should be performed carefully and respectfully and follow safe rules of conduct. Occasionally, we have come across students and teachers who liked to show off their skills at the expense of a partner but this is something that we have only very rarely seen in our own classes.

With very experienced students, there might be a mutual agreement to make the fight a bit more realistic in order to test self-defence skills that might be needed on the street, but even then, all safety precautions need to be in place, students need to be fully insured and the basic rules of combat should be observed. You can find a copy of the international competition rules listed on the website of the British Council for Chinese Martial Arts. Do check your professional indemnity certificate, as your cover may exclude certain types of combat, such as mixed martial arts and kick boxing.

Of course, the most important lessons in a martial arts class are about learning how to avoid getting into a fight in the first place, and not everyone wants to learn to fight anyway. Many people learn Tai Chi as part of their 'spiritual' development, so that's something else that you can offer in your classes, by teaching the meditative and mindful aspects of the art. We will look at that more closely in the final chapter of this book, but first we need to examine the teaching process in more detail.

Step 4

Understand the Teaching Process

We have looked in detail at various methods of communicating your skills and knowledge to your students. In this section, we will look at the overall process of teaching and how people learn, so that you can see all your teaching skills in a broader context.

The Teaching Cycle

Your role as a teacher is to:

- Identify the needs of your students.
- Plan a suitable programme of learning to meet those needs.
- Communicate skills and understanding in a variety of ways to allow every student to achieve their objectives.
- Review the progress of your students at all stages of their learning.
- Provide feedback to your students on their progress.
- Evaluate your own effectiveness, using feedback from learners where appropriate, and use this to enable you to continuously…

- Improve your teaching skills.

This is a continuous feedback loop so that the more you teach and reflect on your practice, the more you learn and the better your teaching becomes.

One of the things you can reflect on right now is how you have learned any difficult skill in the past, such as how to drive a car, knit a jumper or, indeed, perform a Tai Chi sequence. Pick something that you found easy to learn and something you found difficult to learn.

Questions to ask yourself

- For each skill you learned, what made the skill easy or difficult to learn?
- Was there something about the teacher or the methods they used that you found particularly helpful or unhelpful?
- What stages did you pass through on the way?
- Did you eventually master that skill or did you give up at some stage? Why do you think that was?

You will see that learning a skill happens in four distinct stages:

The Stages of Learning

1. **Unconscious Incompetence** - I don't even know what it is that I don't know how to do.

2. **Conscious Incompetence** – I know what it is that I want to do but I don't know how to do it yet.

3. **Conscious Competence** – I can do it when I really think about it.

4. **Unconscious Competence** – I can do it without thinking. (This applies to mastery and also to bad habits).

An instructor helps the student to move from 1 to 4 (but not too quickly).

A trainer takes student from 4 back to 2 and helps them to correct any faults.

A teacher does both and also provides relevant knowledge to put those skills into context and lead the student to a deeper understanding of what they are doing and why.

We do all of these in every class. Our ongoing task, in every lesson, is to establish every student's existing level of skill and help them to move forwards (formative assessment).

We have to find a balance between helping them to:

- gain a mental map of the form and

- improve the quality of their movements within the form, which comes from their understanding of the principles.

The order of a sequence can be learned from a DVD or a clip on YouTube or even from a book. Our main role is to help the student to do the movements correctly, to inspire them and to deepen their understanding of the principles, philosophy and applications of the forms as they go along.

If we go too quickly from 1 to 4, we not only miss opportunities to enrich their experience of Tai Chi but we create entrenched bad habits which are difficult to correct later on.

Formative Assessment - Giving Feedback to Students

This is obviously an important role for any teacher. The whole point of having a teacher, rather than trying to learn Tai Chi from a video, is that a teacher will tell you whether or not you are doing it right and will help you to correct any mistakes.

The manner in which you give this feedback to your students is very important. Whatever you think about their performance, their self-esteem and motivation should be your main consideration. As a good rule of thumb, always start positively, by pointing out what they are doing well, then give helpful suggestions on how to improve. If there are lots of errors, don't bombard them with all of them at once, just focus on one or two major ones and come back to the rest later. Always try to end on a positive note that makes them feel that they are making progress and that success is achievable for them.

Sometimes, focusing on just one aspect, if it is a basic principle such as sinking, can improve a whole host of other difficulties. In the Tai Chi classics, it says: 'If there is a problem with the form, look to the root', so focus on the footwork, stances and posture rather than worry too much about the arm and hand positions. There is also no point trying to get them to use the waist or the dantien if they are not sinking down or if they are leaning forwards, backwards or sideways, or their stance is too narrow, all of which stiffen the spine and prevent the waist and dantien from moving freely.

As we already said in the section on Communication (Step 3), it's best to introduce amendments with "and" rather than "but" since it is human nature to dwell on the negatives, which "but" implies, even when 99% of the form is brilliant. That 1% may need correcting but it's important that the student doesn't take your suggestion for further improvement as criticism.

"And" implies that the form is near-perfect and that a little extra modification will make it even better. For example, you might say something like: "You stepped round into single whip really well and it would be even better if you could relax and settle your weight into your legs a bit more. That will make it easier to turn your waist, so that you feel more comfortable and balanced."

Reserve face palms and gestures involving tearing your hair out for experienced groups of students who know you well and appreciate your sense of humour!

It may be useful to give some kind of written feedback to students now and then. A list of the movements of a form with space for ticks and/or suggested amendments can be very useful for students to take away with them, as it helps them to remember what you have said and also gives them a clear idea of what they are aiming for.

To avoid causing embarrassment by pointing out a student's errors in front of the class, one-to one feedback is ideal. If that's not possible, then you might try telling the whole class to be careful to do whatever it is you want a particular student to do.

The danger with this approach is that the one student who was making this error is probably the least likely to pay attention to your class-wide advice and will continue to make this error, while all the people who were doing it correctly will think you meant them and start making unnecessary changes that actually worsen their form. For example, 'remember to drop your elbows' will probably result in one student blithely keeping their elbows level with their ears while the rest of the class start squeezing theirs in against their ribs in an attempt to keep you extra happy!

Formal Assessment – Judging Levels of Competence

There is no coloured belt system in Tai Chi, except where individual teachers and schools have made up their own grading systems. So don't be surprised if mentioning the coveted 'blue sash' that you worked so hard for brings about blank stares from the rest of the global Tai Chi community.

In our own school, we work to the performance criteria previously set by the Technical Panel of the Tai Chi Union for Great Britain, when they offered qualifications through the Awarding Body NCFE. Although there is no requirement at the moment for Tai Chi students in the UK to undergo assessment for any kind of qualifications, we offer it to our own students on a purely optional basis and find that the levels provide a helpful framework for teaching. While most of our students have no desire to achieve a certificate, others appreciate them as milestones to indicate their progress.

For those students who do wish to be assessed for our qualifications, the criteria at each level are very specific.

We won't list them all here but the following is a very broad outline of the levels we have in mind when recommending appropriate classes to suit each person's current skills and experience. We are not, for one moment, suggesting that our way is the only way or the best way of doing things, we are just sharing this with you in case you find it helpful.

Level 0 – Complete beginners with no prior experience of Tai Chi.

Level 1 – Beginner - People who have been doing Tai Chi for about six months to a year and can perform one short hand form to a very basic level all the way through. They might also be doing a bit of single fixed step push hands, the martial applications of ward-off-roll back, press and push, and a few very basic weapon drills, such as the broadsword (Dao).

Level 2 – Intermediate - People who have been doing Tai Chi for at least a further two years and have learned either two short hand forms or a long form and a weapon form to a good intermediate standard, i.e. following all the main Tai Chi principles relating to posture and movement. At this level, they might also have basic proficiency in some fixed step and moving step push hands drills and a range of martial applications and have a good working knowledge of the main Tai Chi principles.

Level 3 – Advanced - At this level, which can take anything from five years to ten years or more to achieve, depending on the student, they have reached the equivalent of a black belt in other martial arts. They would be performing hand forms and weapons forms in a manner which demonstrates a deep understanding of the Tai Chi principles, including correct breathing and use of internal power, and also be competent in a wide range of martial applications and fully proficient in fixed step and moving step push hands. At this level they may also be practicing San Shou (free fighting) and competition push hands and in our own school they may be invited to train to be an instructor.

Our books are designed to take people through each of these levels, beginning with the free eBooks available on our website (see the Further Reading section at the end of this book).

Your Tai Chi Companion Part 1: Getting Started is for people with no previous experience who are thinking about taking up Tai Chi, looking for a class and wondering what to expect when they go along.

Your Tai Chi Companion Part 2: Moving On is for people with some experience who are working around levels 1 to 2. It includes exercises to help people to understand the basic principles and a troubleshooting guide to help them to identify and correct any unhelpful habits.

Both of these are intended to be like a 'guide at your side' or a helpful friend who knows what goes on in a class and can help you to settle in.

At an advanced level, the first two volumes of our *7 Steps Towards Mastery* series are designed for people wishing to progress towards level 3 and beyond, in hand forms and martial skills, while the third volume, which you are currently reading, is intended for anyone who has reached level 2 or 3 and wants to go on to teach Tai Chi.

In our school, our beginners classes normally consist of students working at levels 0 to 1 and our intermediate classes 1 to 3, though many of our classes are mixed ability and usually have people working at all levels, with experienced students or other qualified instructors providing individual or small group support to any new starters.

Our masterclasses include people who have achieved level 2 as a minimum and are currently working at around level 3 and above, including experienced instructors attending for their own professional development. Those training for competitions meet at other times to further hone their martial skills.

People don't fit well into pre-defined pigeon holes, however, and it may be that, in your own classes, you have some students who are brilliant at forms yet have no desire to practice the martial side, while others may gain medals in push hands competitions despite being unable to remember a sequence.

Assessment should always be there to meet the needs of the student, as an indication of their progress and how to improve, not as a rigid hierarchy that sets them impossible goals to achieve or results in them feeling that they have 'failed' in some way.

We know of schools who have compulsory grading examinations and, in some of them, students are actually asked to leave if they fail a grading!

In one case, qualifications were set up in such a way that the final examination was an inspection of a highly gymnastic form, irrespective of the normal style practiced by the student. This took place under the scrutiny of a panel that included visiting teachers from China and involved an assessment of the candidate's ability to speak Chinese!

We don't have formal gradings with examiners scrutinising every movement from behind a table. All our assessment is informal and continuous, with each skill being signed off when the student is able to practice competently and consistently over a period of time.

If students don't reach the next level, they are still welcome to stay as long as they like if they are still enjoying the classes. We don't enrol them for a particular qualification until they have already reached that level, or we are very confident that they will reach that level soon, so they achieve it very quickly and thus avoid the risk of the whole 'failure' thing!

Gaining Feedback from Your Students

As well as giving feedback to your students, you will need to gain some kind of feedback from them so that you can check that you are meeting their needs effectively. One way of doing this is to ask them, individually and via group discussions, and you will probably gain most of your feedback in this way.

A potential problem with verbal feedback, however, is that students are not always honest with you. They may be too shy to say some things they would like to, or you may not have asked them the right questions to find out what is really on their minds, or they may not want to hurt your feelings by criticising what you do.

A questionnaire, possibly once a term or once a year, anonymous if necessary, can be a useful way of inviting candid comments from your students. You can ask them what they enjoy, what they don't enjoy, how they have benefited from your sessions, what they would like to do in future sessions, and provide a bit of space for free comments or suggestions.

If you work in Adult Education, you will need to produce some kind of student feedback or review sheets for your employers and/or inspectors.

However, if these questionnaires become onerous, they again become barriers to learning and you can lose a lot of students by asking them to fill them in, especially if they have literacy problems or if English is not their first language. You might ask questions verbally to avoid this but that has the disadvantage of putting them on the spot, when they might prefer to make their comments anonymously. Another way to do it is to let everyone take the questionnaires home so that those who are embarrassed about their writing have a chance to get someone else to help them with it, though you might not get all of them back. A potential solution is to use a simple, anonymous tick list such as the one we suggest in Appendix 2.

Teaching on Your Own

No matter how much time you spend helping out in someone else's class, if you want to become an independent teacher, there will eventually come a time when you will need to take a class on your own. You may be a bit apprehensive, but it can actually be a very liberating experience, as you will be in charge of the class and will therefore have more freedom in organising the lesson as you wish to.

You will need to have a clear plan in mind before you start each session. A written lesson plan may be useful, as we will discuss in the next chapter. You will also need to deal with any administrative matters that go along with running a class. These will vary depending on the type of class and type of premises you are using, but they could include, for example: taking registers, opening and locking up the building, liaising with managers and filling in pay claims, invoices or timesheets and keeping these records safely filed away as you will need them when filling in your annual tax returns.

How to feel comfortable when you are teaching

In surveys, psychologists have found that the greatest fear that most people have, even beyond the fear of pain and death, is the fear of public speaking. So if the thought of facing a whole class on your own is scary, take heart from knowing that you're not alone. We've all been there. There are, however, ways of minimising this potential hurdle and setting your feet firmly on your path towards your new career as a Tai Chi teacher.

It can be helpful if your own teacher is willing to 'ease you in gently'. In our school, our trainee instructors regularly help out in class as assistant instructors, so that all the theory discussed during their induction programme can be put into practice. These real-life teaching situations then form a basis for discussions with fellow-instructors and also allow evidence of their teaching skills to be gathered for their instructor's award.

In our Tai Chi classes we try to ensure that anyone wishing to go on to become a teacher has ample opportunities to help individual students on a one-to-one basis and to teach small groups in class. They then begin to lead the warm-ups and cool-downs whenever possible, so that they can get used to being at the front of the class looking out, rather than the other way round, and they can practice speaking to the group as a whole.

We often throw people in unexpectedly rather than let them worry about it for a week or so beforehand. Even if the stress makes their mind go blank and they can only remember a couple of warm up exercises, they can get on and do those and we are there to take over if they run out of ideas. As their confidence grows, they are soon able to take a whole warm-up session with no problems.

Here's a tip! If you are doing warm ups, start with something you are comfortable with such as a few loosening exercises or some stationary 'Zhang Zhong' postures. With the latter, you get to close your eyes for a minute or two, calm down a bit and think about what you will do next. We each have our own preferences. At all times, think 'What do these students need to know or be able to do?' rather than 'What will they think of me?' or 'What skills and knowledge do I have that will impress them?' Taking your attention away from your own ego and focussing it on your students keeps adrenalin to the minimum and automatically ensures that they, and you, have a better learning experience.

We do everything we can to help our instructors to develop their confidence and teaching skills by first of all creating teaching opportunities in classes where they already know everybody. We generally find that all of our students are incredibly supportive of any one of their peers having a go at taking the warm ups for the first time. We then gradually acclimatise them to a wider range of teaching experiences and levels of responsibility, perhaps with new groups that they don't already know, until they are comfortable teaching different types of classes on their own.

We hope that your own teacher(s) will be able to provide you with similar opportunities or that you will have friends and family members who will be happy to let you teach them some Tai Chi. When you are an experienced teacher, perhaps you will be able to offer the same opportunities to your own students who want to become instructors.

If you are nervous to begin with, the best advice is to focus your attention on the needs of the person (or people) in front of you. To be a good teacher, you need to care about how that person is feeling rather than worrying about your own 'performance' and what they might think of you!

The following is how one of us rapidly overcame her fear of teaching.

"One of the most amazing paradigm shifts I ever experienced occurred when I first started teaching Health and Social Care in a College of Further Education and was asked to man a desk during enrolment week. As the first of hundreds of teenagers came flooding into the hall, my heart was pounding with anxiety. What does one say to actual teenagers? I fully expected to be eaten alive until the wonderful lady sitting next to me, an experienced teacher, close to retirement and to whom I am eternally grateful, said: "Oh look at them, poor little dears; their first day at College. They must be scared stiff." That just totally turned it on its head for me. I was no longer a

nervous rookie teacher, I was a substitute mum, and my classes of sixteen to eighteen year olds, who had rarely been to school up to that point, were invariably well attended and resulted in the majority of attendees gaining merits and distinctions and going on to employment or University.

"I found that exactly the same principle applied when I went on to teach managers and top executives who were gathering portfolios of evidence for a national Training and Development qualification. These people were all way above my pay grade and I was quite apprehensive and very much in awe of them until I discovered that all of them were nervous about learning something new and were relying on me, as an 'expert', to explain and show them what to do. So my first function was to put my own feelings aside and put them at their ease. The shift in perspective was quite profound. These days, I just treat everyone the same, whatever role they may play in society. In the end, we are all human; it just took me some time to fully realise that."

You have the Tai Chi Skills and knowledge that the person in front of you wants to learn. You know how they feel because you have been there yourself. Your own experiences of learning Tai Chi can help you to appreciate their difficulties and find ways through them. Sharing your skills with others can be a mutually rewarding and enriching experience.

When you begin to teach on your own, you will need to help students of various ages and levels of ability to do warm up exercises, qigong, hand forms, weapons forms, push hands, martial applications, and cool down activities at the end of a session.

In all of these activities, you will soon develop an ability to recognise:

- what the student needs to learn,
- how much to teach them in each lesson,
- what modifications they need to make to what they are already doing and
- how to provide supportive feedback to motivate, encourage and inspire them and allow them to get the most from their Tai Chi.

You will also need to gain feedback from them in order to evaluate and develop your own effectiveness as a teacher.

The Flexible Approach

As you will have realised by now, teaching is a dynamic, interactive process. You can never really plan exactly what you are going to do and stick to it rigidly, though we will look in detail at the process of lesson planning in a moment.

You will need to constantly modify your approach to meet the individual needs of your students, explaining things again and again in different ways when they seem to be having a mental block, or modifying postures for those who have real trouble due to a health problem or disability.

You will need endless reserves of patience and understanding, for example when students copy your movements exactly and then do something entirely different the next time you see them; often several times over, sometimes for months or years on end. But as well as being frustrating, this is also what contributes to the challenge of teaching Tai Chi Chuan. Ultimately, it can lead to a great deal of satisfaction when a student finally understands what you were getting at and you witness a transformation in their Tai Chi. Even if they never 'get it', you can still take comfort from the knowledge that they have gained pleasure from coming to your classes and that it may have helped them in numerous other ways that you can only guess at.

You will need to have a passion for Tai Chi and a passion for sharing it with others and contributing to their skills, knowledge, pleasure, health and well-being. If this passion is strong enough in you, it will override all the frustrations and difficulties, keep you going through all the repetitions and challenges, and motivate you to constantly develop insights and innovations that will help people to share what you are offering them, while also allowing you yourself to learn and grow from that experience. Ultimately, you will learn as much (or more) from them as they learn from you and this may contribute to your greatest lesson of all: humility. And that's what will make you a great teacher.

Step 5

Have a Cunning Plan!

Before we start this section, we do acknowledge that you might never be asked to write down any kind of plan for any lesson you teach. Then again, depending on where you find yourself working, you could be asked to produce them for every lesson you teach!

So, even if you are never officially required to write one, it is still a good idea to have a go at this skill. It is the basis of sound professional practice and a good habit to get into, especially when you first start teaching. Once you have an overall outline of the content of a session in your mind, you can adapt it at will and it will become second nature to map out the content of a session as soon as you lay eyes on the group you are about to teach.

What is a Lesson Plan?

A lesson plan is just a piece of paper (from a single sheet to no more than 2 or 3 sheets) on which you write an outline of the structure of the session you are intending to teach. It can be a great way to organise your thoughts, maximise the use of your teaching time and make sure you covered all the points you intended to cover, so that all of your students can progress with their learning and you can review how well you have met your aims and objectives.

Ideally, it needs to be fairly brief and in a format that you can read and follow easily to minimise student thumb-twiddling time as you struggle to find your place.

Are lesson plans really necessary?

Whether you see a lesson plan as an asset or a pointless waste of time depends on the subject and type of class you are teaching and your own level of experience and confidence.

For example, if you are teaching an academic subject such as mathematics, geography or science in a school or college, or even giving a talk about a hobby to a local community group, a well-structured lesson plan can be an essential guide. One of us rarely writes down a plan for a Tai Chi class but always has a hand-written set of notes for her philosophy and science lessons.

A written plan allows you to cover your chosen topics properly and to consider the best ways to engage the attention of your students or audience so that they enjoy the learning experience. It can also be invaluable to someone covering your class if you are off sick or on holiday.

On the other hand, if you are teaching a Tai Chi class in which you really don't know who is going to be there that week – you had fifteen experienced students last week but half of them may not turn up this week because it's the holiday season and it's possible that a couple of complete beginners will turn up out of the blue – your well-considered lesson plan may be completely inappropriate for the actual situation you find yourself in. In fact most Tai Chi classes involve having a general outline in mind and then responding to the needs of the students who actually come through the door and doing your best to ensure that everyone receives some appropriate input.

With this in mind, you may think: "Ok let's just do lesson plans in those circumstances where they may be useful and forget about them in the unpredictable sessions where I have to think on my feet as the situation demands".

Well in some classes, such as your own private ones in premises you book yourself, or in some health clubs, this is probably the best way to go, but if you take on a class for a local College of Further Education or other organisation that receives funding from the government, local authority or elsewhere, you will be inspected regularly and your lessons will be observed.

When an Ofsted or local council inspector walks into your class, you will be expected to produce all manner of documentation as evidence of every stage of your delivery of your subject, and lesson plans and schemes of work are the main items they will ask to see.

Bearing in mind that we have just pointed out that producing appropriate lesson plans for a Tai Chi class is well-nigh impossible in the first place, the following guidelines explain how to produce this documentation in a way that will be acceptable to inspectors without giving you a nervous breakdown in the process.

What is a lesson plan for?

The main reason for having a lesson plan is to give you time to think, in advance, about what you want to communicate to your students. You can then decide how you will do that and write this down in a way that is easy to refer to during the session in order to jog your memory. When you first start teaching, this can be like a lifeline that helps you to structure and pace a class and prevents you from stalling in the middle. Although you can be flexible enough to spend some time responding to unexpected questions from students, your lesson plan can help you to avoid getting completely side-tracked and forgetting important things that you had intended to say or do.

The more experienced you become, the less you may need to rely on written plans because you have done it all and said it all so many times before that it is always there in your mind, along with any more recent information and insights you may have acquired. You can become more creative in finding new ways of responding to the needs of students in front of you and imparting your skills and knowledge in a way that works best for them at that moment.

How do you structure a Tai Chi class?

That's up to you, but much will depend on the type of class you are teaching, the number of students in your class, the needs and abilities of everyone present and how much time and space you have available.

A fairly typical one-hour session might start with some warm-up exercises and qigong, followed by some Tai Chi form or push hands instruction with the whole class or in small groups, as appropriate, and end with a cool down or closing meditation to bring everyone together and 'centre them' before they go on their way.

In a longer class, there might be time for everyone to sit down for a short discussion or a meditation in the middle of the session, providing a welcome opportunity for older students, in particular, to take the weight off their feet for a while.

In a very complicated class, with lots of lots of students at different levels, you might have staggered breaks so that some can work with you while others go out for refreshments or practice on their own. In some of our classes, the break gave us the space for experienced students to practice broadsword while beginners went off for a cup of tea or stayed to watch and be inspired.

One potential advantage with a college class is that students typically enrol for a whole term, which means that they all progress together, making it easier to plan a structured course, though you may have an influx of new starters at the beginning of each term.

In some colleges, students may enrol for a full year, allowing you to focus on the needs of the whole class without interruption. Even then, some students may occasionally miss sessions through illness or out-of-season holidays. In the unlikely event that they all attend every session, it is inevitable that some students will pick it up more quickly than others, so you will always need to structure your class in a way that accommodates this diversity of aptitude as well as other individual needs.

Though long and complicated sessions can be daunting, especially when you are new to teaching, they can also be extremely rewarding. A highly complex two-hour weekly class of ours, with seventy students and new people starting at the beginning of every term, continued for over a decade and changed the lives of very many people. Many of those students thrived so well in this learning environment that they reached a very high level of skill and became qualified instructors. If you can rise to the challenge and plan your approach well, your efforts can be very worthwhile.

If you only have an hour and have lots of students, all at different levels and all requiring your undivided attention, you have a strong reason to go to the management and ask for another class so that you can split them into beginners and intermediates, if budget and space limitations allow. However, in a health club, the one-hour very mixed ability class, with new beginners dropping in most weeks, is probably the most likely situation you will find yourself in. You will gradually develop ways of dealing with this. What works quite well for us is to teach one or two moves, principles or applications in detail with the whole class so that beginners can learn the basic structure and principles and, at the same time, more experienced students can revise and correct their form and consider how they might teach it to others when the time comes.

We usually make sure that, in every session, those students who already know a whole sequence have an opportunity to go through the whole thing at some stage in order to retain their 'mental map' and let any newcomers see what a whole Tai Chi sequence looks like. Some might be put off because it looks too hard but others will be inspired and stay with you for years in order to learn how to do it. You can do this at the beginning or end of the session. Doing it at the end is particularly recommended because it gives beginners a chance to see where the bit they have just learned fits in. If the move they just learned is a ward-off, roll-back, press or push, they may be reassured to see that it is repeated several times in the form. When they have been coming for a few weeks, they can join in with the bits they know and feel part of the Tai Chi family.

How to Write a Lesson Plan

There are no hard and fast rules about this. If you happen to be working in a college that has a generic lesson plan format for all staff, you will almost certainly find that it is geared towards academic subjects and may be totally unsuitable for a Tai Chi class. If so, you would need to explain this to your line manager and find an alternative that works for you while also covering the points inspectors want to see.

Don't be afraid to make suggestions. Managers and inspectors alike are all human beings and most of them won't know much about Tai Chi and will therefore appreciate your feedback about how Tai Chi classes work best.

Inspectors are not there to see how well you have complied with the requirements of a piece of paper designed by someone sitting in an office, they are there to see that you have really thought about the individual needs of all your students and you are structuring your sessions in a way that allows you to provide them with the skills and knowledge they need in the best ways possible.

A lesson plan might be very detailed or it might be quite simple and very flexible. We have found that both can be used together in practice: having an overall plan for the standard format of the class – the stuff you tend to do in every session - at the front of your teaching file, and then having a brief but flexible one for the unpredictable aspects on a week by week basis. We will say more about this in a moment.

How much detail will inspectors want to see?

They will want to see:

Aims and objectives for your session and perhaps a link back to what has been done previously.

Equipment required (e.g. CD player/iPod, handouts)

The content of the main part of the lesson. This may be in stages, with a 'consolidation' after each. Each stage might involve a different teaching strategy to sustain interest and cater for different learning styles.

Learning methods used (demonstration, group work, discussion etc.). Inspectors like to see a variety of these to prove that you are catering for people with different preferred learning styles and ensuring equal opportunities for all students by accommodating any special requirements.

The times and duration of each stage of the lesson.

Evaluation: a section at the foot of the page in which you have written what went well on that occasion and what you could do differently next time, to show that you are a 'reflective practitioner' who is constantly developing and improving your practice through experience and reflection.

The Main Part of the Lesson.

Here is an example of how this might work for a two-hour class:

Introduction: including warm ups and qigong

Section 1: Tai Chi form as a class, led by instructor

Consolidation 1: Students do the form, or part of it, on their own to see how much they know and what needs to be worked on today.

Section 2: Split up into small groups of people at similar levels, working on an appropriate task, while the teacher goes from group to group, problem-solving, answering questions and giving instruction and feedback where required.

Consolidation 2: Students come together and have a further opportunity to do the form and the teacher asks questions to test their understanding of the principles or discuss points that have arisen during the session.

Section 3: Sitting meditation or tea break, whole group

Consolidation 3: Opportunity for students to ask questions/share their experiences.

Section 4: Detailed analysis of one posture or principle with whole group.

Consolidation 4: Everyone does form again together, bearing that posture or principle in mind.

Conclusion: 'Cool down': Everyone comes together for closing meditation.

The above outline could form the middle, wide column of your lesson plan, with times allocated for each activity in a narrow column to the left and notes on methods or equipment required in a narrow column to the right.

The above suggestion has worked well for us in practice. However, as we mentioned previously, you might not always have this amount of freedom to design your own layouts. The College you work for may provide you with a couple of ring binders full of instructions on the expectations of the inspectorate and a whole sheaf of 'generic' documents or 'pro formas' to fill in and use in your classes.

Do not be daunted by these!

Have a good look through to see what's there and make sure you fill in any important bits or anything useful that can be adapted to make it work for your class.

Most of it may not be relevant to Tai Chi teachers anyway and may be aimed at those of your colleagues teaching academic subjects, and the specimen Lesson Plans and Schemes of Work may only be suggestions and not be as useful as the customised versions you have developed yourself. Ideally, you can set the whole thing out in a way that works best for you. For example, you might prefer a portrait or landscaped layout, and you might use colour coding, highlighter pens or different font sizes for the things you want to jump off the page at you so you remember to include them in your lesson.

Just be ready to explain this to inspectors and senior staff who are unfamiliar with how Tai Chi teaching works or put a note to that effect in the file with your lesson plans. In general, meeting the needs of your students is always the first consideration.

Aims and Objectives

Aims are the general things your students will wish to achieve by attending this course. For example: to learn a short Tai Chi sequence and understand the basic principles relating to structure and movement.

Objectives are the specific things your students will know or be able to do by the end of each session. For example: to be able to do the movement 'Repulse Monkeys' safely.

Obviously, the various benefits your students may be gaining from an individual session could fill a whole book but you just do the best you can to highlight your main expectations for them here. Write them near the top of your lesson plan in the form: 'By the end of this session, students will…' and list them against bullet points.

A word about Key Skills or Core Skills

Colleges may even insist that you include opportunities for students to improve their 'key skills' in your lessons! These are not the skills that you might expect the average Tai Chi student to be focussed on, such as sinking and rooting, they are universal core skills such as literacy, numeracy and using computers!

You might, very rightly, wonder what on Earth any of that has to do with learning Tai Chi. However, it's something you could well be asked by an inspector and you should have something written down about these aspects of learning in your lesson plans or Scheme of Work; preferably the latter as you then only have to write about them once. (We will look at Schemes of Work in a moment.)

If you think about it for a minute, it might not be as irrelevant as it sounds. For example:

- If someone comes to your class who is not already fluent in your language, they will have ample opportunities to practice their conversational skills by interacting with yourself and other students.

- If you are explaining the distances, angles and structure of the postures and movements of Tai Chi, their knowledge of geometry is likely to increase.

- If you have a website, or recommend YouTube clips for home study, your students will need to be able to use the internet. Most will already be using PCs, tablets and phones for this purpose but if not, local colleges may have 'Computers for the Terrified' courses that you can recommend.

So just put something along these lines in writing so that inspectors can see that you have thought about it and are making a contribution to enriching the overall learning experience of your students.

How can you keep the lesson-planning workload to a minimum?

Tip 1 – Type your overall lesson plan on a word-processor and put in the bits that you do every week as part of the routine, such as warm ups, close up, break, form practice etc., and the times that these normally take place.

Tip 2 – Leave spaces for the variable bits such as the date, number of students present, theme of the lesson or discussion topic, handouts you intend to bring, specific objectives that day and of course the session evaluation bit at the end.

Tip 3 – Print off enough copies for that term, put the session dates on them, stick them in a file and remember to take it with you to your classes.

Tip 4 – Remember to fill in the blank bits by hand whenever you can. For example: 'Go over White Crane again today' or 'JD needs to renew insurance' or 'remind everybody about the half-term holiday'.

That way, you will have a good, basic set of lesson plans to show to any inspector who pops through your door.

How can you use a Lesson Plan in a real class if you don't know who will be there?

One way is to have contingency plans.

Just put one copy of your overall plan in the front of your file, and then use a different type of sheet on a week by week basis.

This can be very simple, with just a few spaces on it labelled: 'New starters', 'Beginners', 'Intermediate', and 'Advanced students' as befits the likely population of your class. Print off a few of these, call them something like 'Needs-specific Learning Outlines' and then, by hand, scribble in a few considerations of what you would like to do with students in each of these categories that week, should any of them arrive. We have offered an example of how you might set this out in Appendix 1.

For example, new starters might need to complete enrolment forms and be introduced to the first couple of moves of a hand form by a more experienced student, while your intermediate students might be moving on to start the broadsword or working on perfecting their footwork. The advanced students might be exploring push hands or fa jing or working towards becoming instructors and be happy to assist the beginners.

The example given in Appendix 1 is of a Needs Specific Learning Outline that we have used successfully for a fairly complex weekly class of ours, with students ranging from completely new starters through to experienced teachers, some of whom have been attending for over twenty years! Your classes are likely to be much simpler when you first start out. Probably you would only need space for new starters, beginners and students with some experience.

However reluctant we may be to fill in these bits of paper, it can be quite a useful exercise, particularly when we first start teaching. Your students may even comment on your remarkable capacity to recall their individual progress week by week. To protect confidentiality, however, only use initials on your lesson plans, not student names, and be careful not to leave your teaching file on the bus.

Practice your lesson planning

You might like to have a go at designing a suitable lesson plan for each of the following sessions:

1. A new two-hour class for 40 adults, aged from 20 to 75, who have just started together with no previous experience.

2. A one hour introductory session for 70 university undergraduates who have no previous experience.

3. A one hour class in a private health club where you have a dozen students who have all been attending regularly for three years, though their levels of ability vary. They have learned one simplified short hand form and are now learning a longer form

4. A one and a half hour class in which there are thirty students on the register but the weekly attendance is around twenty. All are at different levels, as you accept beginners and have new people starting almost every week. Some only stay for one or two sessions but there are people in the group who have been with you for several months and, in some cases, for several years.

5. A one hour class in a private health club which is designated as being for beginners, which means that new people come and go every week but some people have been coming for a few months now and have learned quite a bit of the form. The class is composed of middle-class, middle-aged people who have paid for health club membership and feel this entitles them to your full attention for the whole hour and threaten to

complain to the management if you ask them to practice on their own.

6. A two hour adult education class in which you have:

    - Three students who have been with you for over three years. They have learned two short hand forms and a broadsword form and they would like to do more pushing hands and applications;
    - Four students who have been with you for two years and have one decent short hand form and a bit of another.
    - Twelve students who have been with you for one year and have learned a short hand form to varying levels of competence and want to start learning a new one.
    - Fifty new students, mostly complete beginners but three with some previous experience of other styles.
    - The ages of students in the class range from 13 to 84. They have variable levels of health and fitness and a variety of different reasons for taking up Tai Chi. One person is a wheelchair user.

7. A two hour class in which you have support from two assistant instructors. There are often complete beginners in the class, but there are also people who have been coming every week for anything from one to ten years. There are twenty names on the register but attendance tends to range from three to fifteen. One student has been coming for several years but, having been to a previous teacher, does not listen to any of your suggestions and continues to make the same errors. Another student has been going to another teacher as

> well as yourself, to learn a different style. She insists on practicing what she has learned from that teacher in your class and has recently been teaching some of it to your beginners while you are occupied with other students.

All of these scenarios are based on actual situations we have found ourselves in. There may be many different ways to approach each scenario. We found ways that worked well in each case but other approaches could have been equally successful. We have included them here to give you a feel for the many different challenges you might come across when you are out there working as a Tai Chi teacher. It may seem daunting at first but you may find great pleasure in rising to fresh challenges every day and it is unlikely that you will ever get bored!

In case you are wondering about the 'seventy students' bit, large class sizes tend to occur when a class is offered free, or at a very reduced rate, due to subsidies, and the available space is large enough to accommodate everyone safely. While it might seem logical to turn half of them away, it is worth considering that many people don't know what Tai Chi is, so they come along to a first session out of curiosity and then drop out after a week or two.

If you limit numbers, you could turn away someone who has yearned to do Tai Chi for many years and, given a chance, is likely to stick with it and perhaps become one of the best teachers in the business in years to come. We can remember a class where we had seventy at the start of each academic year, and about thirty stuck with it year after year, some of these eventually becoming great teachers.

What is a Scheme of Work?

In its simplest form, a scheme of work is just a list of what you intend to cover, week by week, with dates on, in order to achieve a particular aim by the end of term/semester.

How to Write a Scheme of Work

For an academic subject or a class in which all your students are at the same level, writing a scheme of work may be quite straightforward. Tai Chi classes, on the other hand, tend not to be so simple. Luckily, the first classes you teach are likely to be composed entirely of beginners, which allows you time to practice your scheme of work writing skills before the next term's new starters arrive and complicate matters.

For example, your aim might be for your group to be able to do the first section of a form by Christmas. You then break it up and say which moves you intend to teach them each week. Then you say what learning methods you will use, so that others can see that you have included a variety of approaches and resources.

For a more complex class, in subsequent years, you will need to have a landscaped document with columns for the intended learning outcomes of beginner, intermediate and advanced students, methods to be used, and perhaps the overall theme of the lesson and any special considerations that week.

Having such an overall scheme can work well, if all goes to plan, but don't be surprised if, a few weeks in, half the class can only remember the first two movements, half a dozen picked it up in no time and are chomping at the bit to move on to the next section, and several more were off sick or on holiday for various bits of it and are trying to catch up or losing heart because they think they are falling behind.

You may then have to sub-divide the group so as not to hold half of them back or demotivate those who are struggling. This is not a failure on your part, it is normal. Just write down what actually happened, all over your shiny scheme of work, rather than becoming a slave to a piece of paper and trying to force your students to meet its demands.

Your Scheme of Work is what you might expect in an ideal world but the sheer human variability of students is the reality of Tai Chi classes. The real art of teaching is not getting everyone to conform to your mould, it's adapting to their individual needs at every stage of their learning. In the end, you are not a general training an army, you are more like a gardener planting seeds and then providing the right conditions in which unique plants can germinate, develop and thrive.

How to Prepare for Inspection

If you are teaching a class in a College of Adult or Further Education, you would be well advised to gather together a few essential documents and keep them together in a ring binder which will henceforth become known as your teaching file or course portfolio. Years ago, one of us used to call this her 'What if I die?' file, since it was the stuff that anyone would need to know about her classes if she happened to get run over by a bus. Since then, these documents have become ubiquitous throughout the teaching profession. They are actually very useful in a variety of circumstances, including times when you are off work sick and others have to cover classes for you and, especially, on those occasions where an inspector walks into your class.

Inspectors can be working for the Government, the local Council, a College you are working for, or anyone else involved in funding your classes. They will want to observe you teaching your class and to have a look at any documentation related to it. It makes life easier for them and for you, if you always have this paperwork to hand in your teaching file.

What to Put in Your Teaching File

As a minimum, you will need:

• Your register of student attendances.

• Your lesson plans for that lesson and the weeks before and after it.

• Your scheme of work.

Ideally, you should also include the following:

Equal Opportunities Explanation

Inspectors like to see that your practice is anti-discriminatory, ensures equal opportunities and overcomes individual barriers to learning, so it's as well to think about this ahead of time and put a statement about it into your file. Usually the College will have an equal opportunities policy that you adhere to anyway but you can mention how you are accommodating individual needs and any disabilities or difficulties your students may have, without mentioning any names of course. For example: 'Two students have hearing impairment, one student has a hip replacement' and how you accommodate these needs.

Describe how the room you teach in has access for wheelchair users or, if not, that you have reported this to your line manager. Anything else you have done, like providing handouts in large type, arranging for an interpreter to assist a student who does not speak English, or any online learning resources you have created to support home study, can all be flagged up here.

Action plans/learning agreements and end-of term questionnaires

You may have to complete these as part of your contract of employment. Often they are fiddly things, several pages long, that have carbon copies, one for the student and one for you that you keep in your file to inform your teaching and show to inspectors.

In our own experience, these forms can, in themselves, form a barrier to learning. As a College-wide policy, they may work well with full-time academic courses which tend to have time allowed for individual tutorials during induction week. In a weekly Tai Chi class, however, sitting down with each student to fill in a form can take hours to accomplish - time in which the rest of the class have to practice on their own without your support. You can imagine how, in a class of seventy students, spending half an hour with each student filling in one of these forms would mean that no actual teaching took place at all that year!

Even if you send students away with forms to fill in at home, most of the forms, and possibly most of the students, won't come back! For some, just the idea of filling in a form, even with your help, is daunting. They came to learn Tai Chi, not to reveal their difficulties with literacy or have their progress recorded in writing.

Obviously, the reason for having these documents is to ensure that teachers don't just turn up and do any old thing, with no regard for the needs of the students. The documentation is intended to ensure that the student is given a chance to let you know what they expect from your course so that you can think about how you can help them to achieve this. The irony is that this documentation, designed to support the rights of students and make sure you are doing your job properly, actually interferes with the rights of students and stops you doing your job properly!

As an alternative that has worked well for us and has been well-received by visiting inspectors, we have devised a one-page document with two columns, each containing an identical list based on common objectives shared by thousands of our students over the years. There is also a space at the bottom for any others that we had not thought of. At the beginning of term, the students tick any of the options in the left hand column that apply to them. At the end of term they use the right hand column to tick all the ones they feel they have achieved. It only takes a few minutes to go through the tick list and our students have been happy to complete them. We have provided an example of how to create such an Initial Learner Agreement and Feedback Sheet in Appendix 2.

From these simple sheets, we know the main areas to focus on with a particular group each term and, at the end of the course, we can see how successful we were in helping each student to meet their personal objectives. We can also produce a brief statistical summary to pass on to managers. Just add up the responses to each question and enter the numbers into a spreadsheet and you can produce simple bar charts or pie diagrams that show you at a glance where your students interests lie and the benefits they have gained from your classes.

These documents should be stored securely, not carried around in your teaching file. Just keep a specimen blank copy and a summary of your findings to show to inspectors if they ask to see them.

Optional Extras

You can also put into your portfolio a few things you are particularly proud of, such as:

- previous inspection reports,
- a copy of the introductory leaflet you give to new students,
- newspaper clippings of your brilliant students doing awesome things,
- a general statement giving a bit of background about the class,
- a brief curriculum vitae listing your impressive credentials,
- one or two handouts that your students have found to be particularly helpful,
- your website address and a list of the online learning resources you provide,

- a copy of your music licence, professional indemnity insurance certificate and martial arts licence,

- a description of the lives your class has changed (without naming names) such as the students who used it against muggers, or those who became instructors and are no longer unemployed.

- anything else you think that the inspector might need to know.

Just don't overdo it. Remember that:

- the inspector will not have time to read an encyclopaedia,

- you will have to carry this file around with you without sustaining a back injury,

- you are providing information to make the inspector's life a little easier.

What To Do if an Inspector Comes to Observe You

- Smile! This is not an ordeal, it's an opportunity to show off your amazing students and let them show someone from the actual outside world how awesome Tai Chi is!

- Welcome your inspector and invite him or her to participate in the class if they want to, or find them somewhere nice to sit and watch. Remember that the inspector may be more nervous and stressed than you are! Theirs is not the greatest job in the world; yours is!

- Give them your file of lesson plans with a fair amount of pride. After all that work - at last - a chance for it to be appreciated!

- Quickly go back to your students and put all your attention on helping them to learn Tai Chi, which is what you are actually there for. Forget about the inspector until they tap you on the shoulder and tell you they have seen enough and are going now.

- If they want to ask questions or give you feedback, they will normally wait until the break or the end of the class. If not, you can ask your students to practice or help each other (peer-assisted learning) while you step outside for a moment, providing it's safe to do so and you are not leaving them to practice push hands or weapons forms unsupervised, in which case you can decline their invitation to leave the room on safety grounds.

- They may also want to speak to your students without you listening, so you may need to go outside and spend a few minutes with your ears burning as your students convey their praise/complaints as they see fit.

- Breathe a sigh of relief when it's over and go about your life again like the world is still turning on its axis and the sun is actually still shining out there somewhere!

- Don't be surprised if your inspector expresses a desire to enrol as a student in your class!

Step 6

Keep it All Legal

In this section, we will look at your legal and professional responsibilities as a teacher. Some of these may be listed in your contract of employment for each company you work for or hire premises from. Since we are based in the UK, much of what follows will be related to the requirements in our country, since these are the ones we ourselves have to comply with.

Other countries are very likely to have similar regulations, so once you have read through this section and understand why these are necessary, you will be able to check out what you need to do in your own state or country.

Professional Memberships and Insurance

To teach any martial art, including Tai Chi, you need to have professional indemnity insurance. In the UK, you can do this through the following organisations, though there are others. To become an instructor member and gain insurance through the BCCMA or the TCUGB, you need to be recommended by an existing member or undertake a technical assessment by their representative(s).

BCCMA - The British Council for Chinese Martial Arts

This is the official, government-approved body for the United Kingdom. If you live in a different country, you will need to find out which governing body covers you.

The BCCMA has lots of other Chinese Martial Arts under its umbrella, as well as Tai Chi, and the sheer number of these members allows them to keep the cost of their insurance down slightly in comparison to elsewhere. There is also an annual membership fee to be paid by the head of the club or school.

Individual licences for your students to practice martial arts (member to member cover) can then be obtained through the BCCMA for a further small fee per student. This covers them if they accidentally injure a fellow student who subsequently decides to sue them. If you only do Tai Chi for health and relaxation, your students should be covered by the public liability insurance of the establishment you work for, but if they are doing push hands, applications or using weapons, or you are running a private class in premises you have hired yourself, they should have BCCMA licenses.

TCUGB - The Tai Chi Union for Great Britain

This organisation has several hundred Tai Chi instructor members, but the overall membership is lower than that of the BCCMA. The overall cost of membership and insurance combined works out roughly the same for each organisation.

They do not offer individual member-to-member licences but there are different levels of cover for instructors, depending on whether or not you are teaching the martial aspects of the art.

The Benefits of Membership

The benefits of joining either the BCCMA or the TCUGB, or both, goes way beyond the provision of insurance. By joining, you become part of a professional body. Since membership is dependent upon recommendation by an existing member or an assessment by the Technical Panel or appointed representative, your membership certificate is equivalent to a professional qualification.

The BCCMA also offers coaching awards, if you wish to undertake them. The TCUGB does not offer assessed national qualifications at this time but there are grades of membership depending on your level of experience, ranging from novice, through advanced to senior instructors who are teaching a full syllabus and have more than twenty years of experience. Your grade is recorded on your membership card and there is an optional certificate available if you ask for one. The TCUGB also provides training and certification for competition judges, as does the BCCMA.

As an additional benefit, your name and grade will be included on the lists of approved instructors on their websites, so that potential students can find you more easily. Their websites also list forthcoming events and you may be able to advertise your own seminars and workshops on the TCUGB website.

Outside the UK

An online search reveals that there appear to be similar non-profit organisations in other countries. These include the Tai Chi Association of Australia, The Taijiquan and Qigong Federation for Europe, The Canadian Taijiquan Federation, and The American Tai Chi and Qigong Association. The ATCQA seems to be focussed on the health side of Tai Chi rather than the martial aspects but the US does have some long-established martial arts associations, including the United States Martial Arts Federation. We can't speak on behalf of any of these organisations, as we are not members of them, but they may well be worth looking into if you live in those countries. There are also various companies offering insurance to Tai Chi instructors worldwide. Our advice would be to shop around and compare what they have to offer.

Criminal Background Checks (Police Checks)

In the UK, all people working with children or vulnerable adults need to be checked by the Disclosure and Barring Service (DBS). Since some of our students could be under eighteen or over sixty or suffering from mental health problems, most employers ask us to have a current DBS certificate. Some of them will arrange it (for a fee of about £30 - £80) and others just require it and ask us to get one elsewhere. This is not easy but it is possible if you do an online search for organisations in your area who will provide this service for other people as well as for their own staff. Outside the UK, you will need to find out if there is any similar requirement for you to prove that you do not have a criminal record.

Even with a current certificate, we would recommend that if you are teaching children, there is always either a parent or, if you are in a school, a teacher present. This precaution is not only an additional safeguard for the child, it is also for your own protection by providing a potential witness who can attest to your professional conduct at all times. If children are left in your charge, you are acting in loco parentis so you must ensure their safety in your classes and also ensure that they get home safely after the class by waiting with them until their parent/carer arrives to pick them up.

Music Licences

Anyone using copyrighted music in their classes or public demonstrations has to be licenced to do so. In the UK, until very recently, there were two main types of licence:

A PPL (Phonographic Performance Ltd) licence, which grants licences on behalf of recording artists and record companies.

A PRS for Music (Performing Rights Society) licence, which grants licences on behalf of composers, songwriters and publishers.

The two types of licence have now been combined into one but this includes tariffs from both.

Obviously, as a martial arts teacher, if you don't use music at all then there is no requirement to have any kind of music licence.

However, if you do like to have a bit of music playing in the background while your students do their forms, then you must always have a current music licence unless you are teaching in a Health Club. Health clubs have to take out a blanket licence which covers all the classes taking place in their establishment, so you don't need one if you only teach in Health Clubs, though some do pass on the charge to their instructors by taking a percentage cut from their wages!

In all other types of premises you may teach in, such as Community Centres or privately hired halls, you will need your own music licence. You pay a fixed cost per class for every single session you teach, currently around two pounds per class. This might not seem much but when you work out how much you actually earn per class after all your travel time, fuel costs, insurance, expenses and overheads, it can be quite a substantial percentage of your earnings.

If you make a living from teaching Tai Chi, with several classes a day, and you multiply that by the number of weeks you teach each class per year, this can soon add up to a four-figure amount.

If you look at the website pplprs.co.uk, you will find that a lot of it concerns the owners of businesses and buildings. Any building where music is played, including background music in bars or shops, has to have a licence. Community centres and halls where you teach may therefore have a licence that covers you but you need to check this. Your classes would come under the tariffs set for fitness and dance.

The law is very specific that any music that can be overheard by anyone else in a public space has to be licenced. So you can play music in your own home or listen to it outside on headphones but if you play it on a loudspeaker where passing members of public, or your students, can hear it, then you need a music licence. This would include parks and other open spaces.

Then again, we have found that there is no need to play music while practicing Tai Chi in the park; the sound of the birds singing is a much nicer accompaniment! Unlike most other types of exercise and dance classes, music is not strictly necessary for Tai Chi and many people prefer to practice in silence.

If you really can't do without music, don't be tempted to ignore the requirement for a licence. If they send out an inspector and you don't have one, or if you fail to renew it before its expiry date, then both you and any company you work for can be sued and prevented from teaching classes, so you really need to have one if you want to use music. Your licence fee may also be increased by fifty percent if you are caught playing unlicensed music and you may need to pay any back fees owing for previous years!

These licences may seem onerous but they ensure that musicians and composers are paid for their work. The licencing bodies do not make a profit; they only operate as collection services and pass on the fees you pay straight to the artists and companies who hold the copyrights.

You can, however, avoid this expense altogether, either by not using music at all or by using royalty-free music, which may be completely unsuitable for Tai Chi. You cannot avoid it by only using Chinese music in your classes, as the licencing requirements are applicable for music produced anywhere on the planet.

Another option is to write your own music. In the end, we composed and produced our own royalty-free music.

In the United States, all Public Performance Rights are handled by three agencies: the ASCAP, the BMI and the SESAC. Elsewhere, you would need to find out the licencing regulations in your own country.

Conduct Expected by Employers

As a teacher, normal professional conduct is expected, including actually turning up to teach your classes and being reasonably punctual, i.e. there on time or a little before unless there is an emergency, and letting them know at the earliest opportunity if there is a problem. If you need cover for absences, you will need to arrange this yourself, since there are very few Tai Chi teachers around and, of those, most of them may be teaching a different style to yours.

Employers are unlikely to know much about Tai Chi and might, with the best of intentions, ask a Wu Style teacher to cover a Yang Style class, for example, resulting in a group of very confused students and a perplexed instructor. It can be helpful to get to know other instructors in your area and share contact details so that you can help each other out if necessary.

Some places have dress codes but obviously the common sense approach is to be user-friendly for your students (clean and sweet to push hands with) if possible.

Accounts and Self-Assessment Tax Returns

In the UK, you will need to register with your nearest Tax Office as Self-Employed (even if you also have full time or part-time paid employment) if you are not already registered. You will be responsible for completing an annual Self-Assessment Tax Return form and for keeping accurate accounts of your earnings from any classes you teach. These may be audited at any time, along with all the evidence of your income and outgoings that supports them.

To register you just phone your local Tax Office and arrange to get a Unique Tax Payer Reference number. You can then complete your tax return online. You will be given a code and password to access the form on the HMRC website. This is very user-friendly and easy to complete. There are separate sections for your paid employment (you just type in the details from your P60 on these) and your self-employment (you just tell them how much money you made altogether [turnover] and how much your expenses were). When you've answered all the questions, you just press a button and your tax for the year is calculated there and then and you can submit it to them and pay your bill online.

Before you do this, you need to get your accounts up to date. Accounts for each year (from 6th April to 5th April the following year) need to include your income from each class and all your expenses such as fuel, bus fares, music you bought for your classes, professional memberships, licences, insurance, clothes or equipment for your teaching, stationery, photocopying, postage, website costs and anything else that you have paid for in order to do your job. You need to keep receipts for all these things and store them safely in case an auditor asks to see them.

You can get complicated business accounts packages but unless you go into business big-time, set up a company and employ staff, you don't really need these, or an expensive accountant. As a sole trader, you can just set up a simple Excel spreadsheet which does the job adequately, providing your maths is OK and you check it very, very carefully before completing your tax return. At any time, an auditor may ask to see your accounts for that year or for previous years, together with evidence of your earnings and expenses, so you need to keep hold of all your receipts, invoices, registers and anything else that may be relevant.

For most classes, your evidence of income will be the copies of your invoices, but if you go on the payroll of a College you will need your P60 or equivalent and you will need to enter your earnings and any tax paid as 'employment' rather than 'self-employment'. If you have hired premises yourself, you will need proof of everything your students have paid, usually recorded on your register, and anything you have paid out for hiring premises. So don't throw anything away! Update your accounts and file all your invoices and receipts regularly to avoid a last-minute panic the week before your tax-return is due.

Other Legal Requirements

By following the advice we gave at the start of this book, you will naturally have an approach to teaching that is in keeping with the requirements of the UK Health and Safety at Work Act, the Equal Opportunities Act, the Data Protection Act and the new General Data Protection Regulation (GDPR) or, if you live elsewhere, any similar legislation in your own state or country, though you can check these out to make sure.

So now, if you're ready, let's get started setting up that class!

Step 7

Get Started!

Once you have decided that you are ready to take on a class of your own, and you have got yourself appropriately checked, insured and licenced, the next question is: what sort of class will you teach and where?

Where to Teach and What to Expect

The following is a list of possibilities that you might want to consider. We have been very honest about the potential benefits and drawbacks of each, based on our own experiences over many years. Our intention is not to put you off but to give you a realistic idea of what to expect before you commit yourself to taking on a class. This is all stuff that we would have found very useful if we had known it when we first started.

Hired Premises

Hired premises, such as church halls, dance studios, community centres or dojos, are usually very expensive. You have to have lots of students in order to pay for the hall and, if you are lucky, have a bit left over as income.

Even with a decent sized group, if a few people are absent that week, your income will decline or disappear altogether, since you still have to pay for the hall. On some weeks, you may even find that you don't meet your overheads at all and you are therefore paying for the privilege of teaching.

You have to do this type of class for the sheer love of it and your students rather than as a business venture, otherwise it probably is not worth your while. You need to check that you are meeting all your overheads, not just the room rental, especially if you have to travel a long way to get there, or you can easily be running at a loss without realising it.

You also need to keep accurate registers and records of who has paid what. These are auditable documents.

One way to try to make sure that you can afford to hire the hall is to ask your students to pay up front for a block of lessons, non-refundable if they don't show up. Alternatively, they could set up a direct debit. You can offer a discount as an incentive for this.

It is also extremely helpful if the person you hire the room from is kind enough not to charge you if a class is unavoidably cancelled, due to heavy snow, for example.

On the plus side, if you hire your own hall, you are completely your own boss and you can organise your classes in whatever way you choose.

Colleges of Further Education

To work in these settings, you need to apply to a local College or answer their job adverts, which may be in a local or national newspaper or on their website. Even if there is nothing advertised, you might try writing to their Human Resources department, or to whoever is in charge of planning the curriculum in the Sports and Leisure department, to ask if they have ever considered offering a Tai Chi class. Do check first to see if they already have Tai Chi courses running at the college!

This is normally contract-based employment for which you go on the company payroll. Your money is spread over a year and you get a monthly pay slip. In the UK, it is very poorly paid compared with other establishments and, for this, you need to do all the lesson plans and schemes of work discussed in the previous chapter and have your lessons observed by College, Council and Government inspectors at regular intervals. The record for us was all three in the same fortnight!

To gain this type of employment in the UK, if your initial interview is successful, you will normally need to have registered teacher status with the Department for Education. You may have to undertake a medical examination and you will also need a current criminal background check (DBS).

You may also need to gain a Cert Ed, PGCE (Post Graduate Certificate in Education) or equivalent qualification, in order to gain professional teacher status, and you may not receive the full (though still modest) rate of pay until you qualify! If you were to pay for a degree course on your own, current fees in the UK are around nine thousand pounds per year, but it may be possible for an employer to subsidise your studies as part of your professional development.

On the plus side, since you are an actual employee, you may be entitled to sick pay and holiday pay and be able to have national insurance and pension contributions deducted from your wages. This can give you a certain amount of job security, compared with all your other options, but you will have to think long and hard about whether it is worth it to you.

Local Authority Sports and Leisure Centres

This may vary depending on where you live and the kind of class you are teaching. If you are hiring a room or hall from the local council and finding your own students, it may be worth your while if you can attract enough students to make it viable. If you are offered a class organised by the centre, it is possible that you may find that your income barely covers your travel expenses, though you might still consider it if you love teaching Tai Chi so much that you are not bothered about the money and have an alternative source of income to meet your living requirements. In our own area, the last we heard was an offer of £12 per hour, which would have resulted in zero actual income or less once overheads were deducted.

Private Health Clubs and Leisure Clubs

Often this kind of employment is acquired by invitation due to your reputation in the area, or by referral from your own instructor or a colleague, if there is a class they need to pass on. However, if there is a Health Club close to you that does not have Tai Chi on their list of classes offered, you can always send them a CV/résumé and a letter suggesting that you would be happy to offer one.

You work for the club as a freelance instructor and submit a monthly invoice. Your money is normally paid directly into your bank every two to four weeks. Classes are closed without notice if student numbers fall so there is no job security in this line of work and you sometimes have to modify your teaching ideals in order to keep the numbers up, otherwise you (and they) will not have a class!

Members of health clubs may be paying out a lot of money for their gym membership and, because of that, they may have very rigid demands on their teachers and expect your full attention throughout every session, rather than splitting into groups doing different activities. You can, of course, suggest that all your students spend some time doing it on their own so that feedback can be given and corrections made, but it has to be said that this particular strategy has been known to result in a spectacular fall in student numbers on certain memorable occasions! How far you are prepared to modify your approach to keep a class viable is entirely up to you.

The advantages of working for a health club, however, are considerable:

- You will be teaching existing members of a club, therefore you don't have to advertise your class, as it will be on the timetable and hundreds of people will already know that it is there.

- Most of your students will have already paid for membership or pay per session at reception, so you will not need to collect in money yourself but will receive a fixed fee, irrespective of how many students attend.

- There is not, normally, a requirement to have written lesson plans or schemes of work, or to be inspected, as your professional integrity and competence are usually assumed.

- At the discretion of the manager, you might also have access to the gym or other facilities at a reduced rate; though this is a concession, not a right.

- Rates of pay tend to be fairly reasonable. In our area this is around £25 per hour but of course you would still need to do a realistic costing of mileage and other overheads to check that this worked out at the minimum wage or above. If not, it may still be worth your while if free or discounted gym membership is included.

Community Groups

Older people's groups and care establishments may hire you by private arrangement. They find the premises and you invoice them for your fee, usually once a month. You need to keep careful records and submit copies of your invoices to make sure you get paid for your work. Some of them are very slow to send out cheques. Some pay directly into your bank account.

Often you will have to collect the class fees from your students at the start of every lesson and hand it in, weekly or monthly, along with your invoice and registers, and the office you hand it in to may be in a different part of the city to the place where you teach.

You may also have added responsibilities such as collecting keys for opening up and locking up the premises.

An advantage of this type of class is that the group may receive funding, which allows them to pay you the going rate while keeping the costs down for students, making it affordable for people on a very low income.

Other advantages are that the organisers will hire premises for you and they will not require you to produce schemes of work or lesson plans. You are simply a trusted professional and how you structure your classes is up to you.

Your fee is negotiated privately between yourself and the organiser and will depend on whether or not they can afford to hire you and how valuable they consider the service you are offering to be.

Think About Specialties

As a Tai Chi teacher, you will need to be flexible enough to help a wide variety of people to meet whatever needs and aspirations they come to you with. There are some specialist areas of Tai Chi teaching that may require a bit of thought before embarking on them. Here are a few examples:

In a typical class in the community there may be students of all ages from nineteen to ninety-nine, but sometimes you may be asked to put on a class especially for children or older people. There are some fairly specialised skills and considerations required for teaching older people and children.

You may also be asked to set up a few sessions for a particular group of patients in a hospital or a medical centre. Such groups might include heart patients, stroke patients, or people with mental health problems, diabetes, arthritis or Parkinson's Disease; ante-natal or post-natal classes or falls prevention for people with mobility problems. You might be asked to teach in a prison, which one of us did, very successfully, for many years.

You may even find that you have particular skills that enable you to specialise in a particular area. You may, for example, already work in the health sector as a nurse, doctor or physiotherapist, or you may be a regular school teacher who wants to add Tai Chi to your curriculum, or a probation officer thinking about setting up a Tai Chi group for ex-offenders, or a care worker in a residential home looking to enhance your activities programme.

Teaching in Hospitals and Community Health Groups

In the UK, classes in medical settings may be funded by the National Health Service or you may work for a private health care provider. NHS or Primary Care Trust funded classes may be quite well paid but they may involve considerable paperwork. In our own experience, this has sometimes meant providing a detailed rationale for every aspect of our teaching and regular reports on the progress of groups or individual students, either monthly or after each session, in order to justify continued funding.

Doing this without compromising the right to privacy of our students was a huge challenge in some cases. If you find yourself in this situation, we would suggest that you do everything in your power to keep such data anonymous and detail to a minimum. We have refused, for example, to ask our students to fill in parts of learner questionnaires that ask for their height and weight. Such details are irrelevant unless there is a specific medical reason for providing them; for example if students have joined the class specifically to help with weight reduction or if the group consists of very ill patients whose weight is being monitored to prevent a decline in their condition. Even then, we feel that such monitoring should be undertaken elsewhere by a medical professional and not by their Tai Chi teacher.

In view of cuts to funding of public services in the UK, it is likely that classes in hospitals may be fewer in the future but this would be unfortunate in view of the widely-recognised health benefits of Tai Chi, which could, potentially, save the NHS considerable amounts of money by preventing a host of physical and mental illnesses. More importantly, it could improve the quality of life for so many people that we would encourage as many good teachers as possible to pursue this line of work, despite its many challenges.

Teaching in Hospices

If you are retired or have alternative means of income and sufficient time available, you might consider offering to work in a charity-run palliative care setting on a voluntary basis. Potentially, you might be able to make a significant contribution to the mental and spiritual well-being of people nearing the end of their lives.

However, as always, do remember that you are there to respond to the actual expressed needs of your students and respect their personal beliefs. Some charitable organisations running hospices may be suspicious of Tai Chi in case it is a religion. Obviously it isn't but if you have a personal leaning towards Taoist or Buddhist philosophies, for example, it would be inappropriate to overemphasise them in such a setting.

Teaching in Prisons

This is another area which is potentially very rewarding in terms of the satisfaction it can offer to know that you are providing a service that could potentially help individuals to change their lives and reduce their probability of reoffending.

Rates of pay can be worthwhile, as befits the level of perceived risk involved, though you might want to do it free of charge for altruistic reasons. If you are thinking of taking on a class in a prison, it's worth knowing that a small group in a small room is preferable to thirty people in a large sports hall with noisy fans round the ceiling and a dozen guards around the edges of the room. We have found that inmates benefit from being able to share in discussions with you rather than just follow instructions on how to do Tai Chi.

The meditative aspects were found to be particularly beneficial, with many people discovering how to find a handle their emotions by stepping back, quietening the mind and resting in the present moment. Students frequently reported feeling better, sleeping better and gaining more control of their temper and aggressive inclinations and several told us that they may never have committed the offence that landed them in prison if they had done Tai Chi or meditation years ago.

Teaching Older People and People with Disabilities

You may be asked to teach a group of able-bodied over-sixties in a community centre, or a lounge full of confused and mostly sleeping ninety-plus year olds in armchairs in a care home. The skills you need will be very different for each of those settings.

We have already seen that a range of physical disabilities can be accommodated in most classes.

Visual and hearing impairment does not need to be an obstacle to learning Tai Chi. Students of any age may have varying degrees of visual or auditory perception so, in any class, you can't always assume that everything you say will be heard or that everything you do will be seen by every student. Your task as a teacher is to find ways to ensure that everyone has an equal chance to share the knowledge and skills you are explaining or demonstrating.

For a student of ours who was completely blind, this involved describing the actions in much more detail than we normally would and, with his permission, taking his hand and gently placing it in the correct position, if required. As we said in the earlier section on equal opportunities, by the end of the year, this young man had a better form than anyone else in the class. Disability does not have to be a barrier to learning.

For students with hearing impairment, ask them what works best for them. They may ask you to speak more loudly or clearly, or turn the music down. For people with a hearing aid, any kind of music can interfere with the electronics and create a loud buzzing noise. They may want to stand where they can read your lips, or they may be content to just watch your movements and copy them carefully. By so doing, they may learn it better than the rest of your students who are busy blissing out with their eyes closed and only want you to do it with them for the company! Again, never make assumptions or stereotype anyone. Individuals will always surprise you!

If your students can walk, whatever their age, and whatever the setting, then to all intents and purposes you will be teaching an ordinary Tai Chi class, and indeed, we often have a few people in their eighties and nineties in our classes and one of them is now an instructor. Even so, you need to be especially aware of any medical problems they may have, such as arthritis, heart conditions, hip replacements or knee replacements, and make sure that they learn Tai Chi safely.

Some students might have difficulty remembering the sequence, but do remember that this stereotype does not fit all older people, some of whom are fitter and brighter than many people half their age. We have had people in their nineties who remember sequences better than university lecturers in their forties!

We have also had classes of people with learning difficulties and/or disabilities who have picked it up more easily than the carers who accompanied them and primary school children who learned it more quickly than qualified martial artists and physiotherapists. It is pretty much impossible to categorise people, so never make assumptions about anyone; just adapt your teaching to their individual needs and capabilities.

For students who can stand but are unable to walk around, qigong is particularly useful. Many older people enjoy qigong exercises. As well as the popular sets such as the Eight Brocade, and stationary Zhang Zhong postures, you can isolate individual Tai Chi moves as Tai Chi Qigong.

Students who cannot stand may be able to do the upper-body movements while sitting in a chair or wheelchair. Our students have included a young gentleman with no legs who could perform an upper body version of the Beijing 24 step Taiji sequence really well. He could still use his waist and dantien, so the absence of legs did not prevent him from enjoying Tai Chi and developing internal power.

Teaching in Residential Care Homes

Chair-based exercise in a residential home is more challenging for you as a teacher, even though you may be sitting down during the session. The following discussion is not intended to put you off, just to prepare you for the realities you might encounter if you take on a class in a Care Home, based on our own experience. In view of the good it can do, it is well worth the effort so don't give up and think that you are wasting your time.

In some homes, or sheltered housing units, the residents are bright, alert and enthusiastic and it is just like teaching any other Tai Chi class, even though some or all of your students may need to do the exercises while sitting down, due to limited mobility.

The real challenge is when residents are less able to participate due to health problems, confusion, tiredness, the medication they are taking, or general frailty. You need vast reserves of empathy and patience to provide them with a meaningful and helpful experience. It must also be said that you are not there to make them do some exercise, though you might encourage and inspire them to do so. It is important to respect the wishes of individuals as well as doing your best to help carers to provide a range of activities for their residents.

In some cases, if residents just want you to go away and leave them in peace, it may be kinder to do so than to keep waking them up and trying to get them to do a bit of Tai Chi.

If your students are awake, this is an advantage. If they are aware of your presence, it is even more encouraging, and if they are willing to look at you and attempt to copy what you are doing, you have a fighting chance of providing them with some exercise and enjoyment.

You will need to speak to the manager before you start and ensure that the rest of the staff know what to expect, so that they don't serve tea right in the middle of your seated meditation or take your most interested student out for their bath. Even then, you can expect that, in any session, your lesson is likely to be punctuated by requests to be taken to the lavatory and you may need to go looking for a carer to help with this before you can continue.

If possible, enlist the help of one of the carers to sit in on the session in readiness for such occasions and to give physical support to anyone who needs it, such as those who have had a stroke and can't lift an arm by themselves. The best idea is to agree this with the manager before you take on the job.

This may be possible if the staff are committed and know the value of what you are doing with their residents and have the time to help but the reality is that your session might be an opportunity to catch up with making the beds or having a staff meeting or a well-earned break. Every Care Home is different, and much will depend on the overall ethos of the establishment and the mental and physical condition of the people who live there.

It is unlikely that very elderly or poorly students will wish the session to last longer than 30 to 45 minutes, and the actual exercise bits are best punctuated with other things, such as a Zen story, a meditation, or a gentle hand massage to stimulate the acupuncture points and increase the flow of Chi to the extremities in order to ease their arthritis, for example.

As with most types of exercise, aim to improve their general strength, flexibility and circulation. As well as doing gentle arm and hand movements from a Tai Chi form or Qigong set, do some exercises that allow them to turn their waist, raise their toes or heels, if possible, and perhaps even lift one foot at a time off the floor and stretch their leg out in front of them.

One of the main dangers of sitting in a chair all day, every day, is that fluid can collect in the legs (oedema/edema), leading to all kinds of problems with the skin and circulation, from leg ulcers to deep vein thrombosis, so anything you can do to help them to improve their circulation will be appreciated. In one home, after just one lesson, the residents surprised everyone by remembering the exercises they had been shown and practicing them every day while watching television.

A good knowledge of physiology is useful and a full police check will be needed before you take on such a class, as older people constitute 'vulnerable adults'. More than this, you will need endless patience, a sense of humour and a real love of older people and a desire to provide them with some pleasure in a potentially less than stimulating day, if you are to take on this challenging role.

When you notice, over the weeks, their increasing mobility, motivation and engagement with what you are doing, it can be very satisfying and well-worth the effort. Age is the great leveller and in our old age it will be people like ourselves, and the great army of carers who have a genuine desire to make other people happy, who will make all the difference to our quality of life in our final years.

Teaching Children

At the other end of the spectrum, you might be invited to teach in a school. This can be fun but it is very demanding and will depend a lot on the age of the children, how well behaved they are and how much energy and enthusiasm you have at your disposal.

For example, you may be asked to run an after-school club once a week, or to participate in a school health day by going into a primary school and teaching every class in turn and then staying behind to teach the staff!

This can be very successful, but your approach will need to change as you move from the reception class upwards.

For younger children, half an hour is probably sufficient, perhaps 45 minutes for the top class and an hour for the staff. Most children are completely turned off by the slow movements of Tai Chi and get excited about anything Karate-like that makes them feel that they are doing a 'proper martial art' which gives them a bit of kudos with their mates. Lots of punching and kicking repetitions across the room, shouting 'hwa' on the way and demonstrating a few jaw-dropping fa jing moves can help to engage their interest and establish rapport.

Starting off with a bit of bowing and an explanation of the need for respect is very useful in terms of establishing the ground rules and you can also do some stationary qigong postures disguised as a game of statues to calm everyone down and keep their attention focused.

The youngest children may enjoy developing Tai Chi qualities by pretending to be a bear, a snake, a tiger, an eagle and a dragon and the older children may enjoy waving hands in clouds and discovering that Tai Chi is a powerful type of Kung Fu!

You will need to have had a clear, recent police check but it is also advisable to have a member of school staff, preferably the class teacher, with you during the session to help maintain good behaviour and also as a witness that your conduct has been professional throughout. You will need to be good with kids of all ages and sensitive to their needs and abilities. However, it is wise to refuse to teach a class where you are left on your own with a large group of hyperactive nine year olds who run riot around you making Bruce Lee noises and trying to punch and kick each other while the rest of the staff retire to the staff room for a rest after a hard day and leave you to it!

One strategy for coping with such a lively group is to play down the martial art bit and do the Zhang Zhong statues thing for a while or have a competition to see who can hear the pin drop, then sit them all down for a five minute meditation, until they are quiet enough to pay attention and do a bit of actual Tai Chi. In one class, we sat and watched the ripples settle in a bowl of water and compared this with how thoughts can settle down in the mind. The children really enjoyed this, as long as each of them had a turn to pour the water into the bowl!

In general, we have found primary school children to be very attentive and respectful. In one school, after being told that they didn't have to bow to us as a sign of respect unless we had earned that respect, the following week we found them bowing to us as we walked across the playground on the way in!

Providing a small certificate at the end of the course is a great way to boost their self-esteem (as long as everyone gets one and nobody is left out) and you may just spark an interest that will last a lifetime.

Finding Your Students – or helping them to find you!

It's great to open a shop, stock it with the best quality produce and then wait for eager customers to walk in off the street. However, if your eager customers don't know where to find you, or even that you exist, you may find yourself with lots of free time on your hands and no means of paying the rent. So how can you let people know where you are and encourage them to come along to your classes?

Here are a few suggestions and our thoughts about each, based on our experience.

Posters and Business Cards

In over thirty years of teaching, we have put up lots of (we think!) awesome posters in local shops, libraries and elsewhere, yet we can honestly say that we don't recall ever having a student say to us that that they came along in response to one of our posters! Our advice would be: save trees, though it may be useful to have a poster in a Community Centre or Church Hall where you have a new class starting. Occasionally though, we have had someone turn up after taking our business card from a health club reception desk. It is also useful to have a supply of these if you are rushing from class to class and someone asks for your website address or contact details. You can also give them to your students to pass on to interested friends.

Website

This is the way to go these days. If you don't have a website, then you simply don't exist in the minds of anyone with a computer, smartphone or similar electronic gadgetry. Once you have a website, it's important to keep all the class details up to date to avoid people turning up at the wrong time or at the wrong location or to a class that has been cancelled. We can also testify, from our experience, that it is fairly unhelpful to inadvertently type next year as the start date for your new class!

Having your own website is also a great way of providing learning resources for your students.

It might also be possible for the Community Group, Church or whatever other organisation you hire your hall from to put your class details on their website or in their newsletter

Professional Memberships

As you saw from the previous chapter, you will need to join an appropriate governing body so that you can meet legal requirements for professional indemnity insurance. A bonus here is that most of these organisations will list you on their website and also refer on any enquiries they receive for a registered instructor your area.

Personal Recommendations and Referrals

Many of our students initially came along after hearing about us from a friend who was already coming to our classes. Many others were referred to us by their doctor or physiotherapist who had noticed improvements in patients who were coming to us already.

In other cases, Community Groups have recommended us to similar groups in the area or asked us to put on another class. In our experience, it is much easier to start a class for a group of people who want a Tai Chi teacher than to set up a class in some random place and then look for students who might want to come along to it. Once you have established a reputation as a good teacher, people are more likely to seek you out.

A word of warning, however, is that we often have requests from companies who want us to travel to remote locations and provide tuition for reluctant staff at unsociable hours of the morning, before work, in a totally impractical space, and at a price unlikely to include more than our bus fare.

Many want us to do a class or demonstration free of charge in the belief that it will boost our public profile and will be an excellent way of marketing our services! The fact that this kindly-suggested marketing strategy would in no way contribute to paying our mortgage seems not to occur to them, so we usually have to respectfully decline their invitation. We have, however, taught some long-running classes for several years, free of charge, or taught together even though only one of us was getting paid, just for the love of the students.

In the end, it's your decision. We are only warning you here so that nobody takes advantage of your good nature.

One consequence of teaching for next to nothing is that it sets a precedent that can affect what is offered to other instructors in the area and undermine the perceived value of Tai Chi generally so don't be afraid to ask for what your services are worth.

Inheriting Classes

Occasionally, a teacher might move to another area, leaving a group of students without anyone to teach them, in which case they, or their students, might approach you to take over the class. This can be a great opportunity but it can be tricky, even if you teach the same style of Tai Chi. Your approach will, almost invariably, be different from that of your predecessor and it may take a while for the group to get used to you, if they don't leave immediately at the first sight of you! Our advice would be to show respect for their previous teacher and their teaching without compromising your own integrity or the Tai Chi principles; a difficult line to tread but possible with tact and perseverance. We have some long-running groups that we inherited in this way.

Existing Audiences

In health clubs, your new class might become part of a programme of activities for hundreds of members who are already looking to try something new. This means that you don't need to do any advertising yourself, but don't get too complacent. If the members don't like what you are doing, they will not come to your classes and, as we said above, most clubs have a policy that if numbers drop beyond a certain level, your class is removed from the programme at that point, without notice.

Another option could be to teach your workmates in a suitable space during your lunch hour; in fact several of our instructors got started this way. There may be other places you can think of to teach that we have not mentioned. The possibilities are endless. Wherever there are people and a bit of space to practice, there is a possibility that some of them may want to learn some Tai Chi.

Financial Considerations

When you begin to teach on your own, you will need to consider all of your expenses, including insurance, licences, travel and any other necessary costs, before negotiating a price and agreeing to take on a class. Always think very carefully about the financial side. However much you love teaching Tai Chi, you need to make sure that you make some kind of income and avoid losing money.

As a freelance instructor, you are only paid for the hours of class contact time. When you consider the travel time between classes – time during which you are not able to earn any money – and you also consider the cost of all your licences and other expenses, you will see that what seemed to be a good rate of pay can work out at less than the minimum wage!

A worked example

We had a look at how much you would earn, as an hourly rate, if you accepted an offer of £20 per weekly class for a group located at a venue ten miles from your home, running for three ten-week terms per year.

Payment per session = £20

From this, deduct:

Music Licence = £2 per session

Professional Indemnity Insurance = £84 spread over 30 weeks = £2.80 per session

Fuel costs for 20 mile return journey at standard mileage rate of 45p per mile = £9 per session

So your actual income = 20 – 2 – 2.80 – 9 = £6.20 per session.

But there is an hour before and after the class during which you are driving, setting up your class, locking up and returning keys, handing in money collected or answering questions from students who stay behind to talk to you. So overall, your earnings from the class are spread over a three-hour period, bringing your actual rate of pay to £2.06 per hour before tax!

This costing would apply if this was the only class you were teaching. Having lots of classes reduces the amount of insurance you would deduct per session and having a class nearer to your home would reduce your fuel bills and travel time, as would teaching two classes close together, so that you could travel quickly from one to the other without returning home and going back again.

Based on the above example, asking for £30 per session would increase your earnings to £5.40 per hour, which is still less than the UK minimum wage for an unskilled worker over the age of twenty-five: currently £7.83. To earn this, you would need to be receiving around £40 per hour. Moreover, you may have put in twenty years or more of training to learn your Tai Chi skills and perhaps have professional post graduate teaching qualifications as well, so you are hardly an unskilled worker.

Other considerations

You also need to bear in mind that, for most types of class, as a self-employed person:

- You will only be paid for those sessions that you teach and not for holidays, periods of sickness or weeks when the class is cancelled, perhaps due to a faulty heating boiler, flood damage or other problems. There are several times a year when many places shut down for a few weeks, including every time it snows if you are teaching elderly students, or the hall may be used for other purposes, such as holiday play groups or concerts. You have little or no income during these periods, so your hourly rate during normal weeks has to be sufficient to tide you through these times as well.

- You will not be paying into a work-related pension scheme, so you need to bear this in mind when planning for your retirement and find a suitable private pension scheme instead. Payments into private pension schemes are recorded on your Self-Assessment Tax Return and do confer a small tax advantage.

The bottom line

- Don't feel guilty for asking for what you are worth.
- If you agree to do a class for free, as we often have, remember that you still have all your overheads so you are not breaking even; you are paying them for the privilege of letting you teach them, rather than earning a living.
- There may be more money available but if you don't ask, you will never know. Community groups may be receiving funding from elsewhere and can therefore keep down costs to students. Even when the students are paying for the class, if you have a large enough group, you may still be able to charge a realistic rate for your services. Don't make assumptions that everyone needs you to keep the cost to a minimum.
- If you accept a very low rate, this sets a precedent that affects all other instructors in the area.
- To make a decent living from Tai Chi, as your only source of income, you would have to be doing four or five classes a day, with most of your classes close to home, and charging a realistic fee for your services.

We're not trying to put you off teaching Tai Chi but just advising you not to give up your day job until you have done all the calculations and shared these calculations with any future employer as an up-front costing.

To teach Tai Chi, you have to love what you do and the people you do it for. As a supplement to your normal income or pension, it can work out very well but if you want to earn lots of money and have job security, Tai Chi teaching alone might not be your first choice of career! On the plus side, wherever you go in the world there may be people who appreciate your skills and would like to learn from you. Their numbers may be small but the satisfaction you gain from teaching them will be immeasurable.

Checklists

Essentials:

1. Get the Tai Chi skills and knowledge (Walk the walk – no shortcuts!)

2. Read this book.

3. Get insurance through an appropriate governing body.

4. Find a place to teach.

5. Find some students who want you to teach them!

6. Do a risk assessment.

7. Get started.

8. Have a great time!

You might also need to:

- Get permission to teach from your own teacher.

- Have a criminal background check (DBS) done.

- Find suitable music and a licence to use it.

- Attend a first aid training course.

- Type up a health and safety policy and equal opportunities statement.

- Complete a government-approved professional teaching qualification.

Optional extras

- Set up your own website.

- Advertise your classes on other websites such as Tai Chi Finder.

Other advice

- By all means, take your martial arts seriously – but don't take yourself too seriously or overestimate your own importance.

- Don't set yourself up as a guru or sifu or devise some other illustrious title that sets you on a pedestal above your students.

- Care for your students, be a friend and a guide, but keep your professional distance and integrity.

- Explore the spiritual aspects if you choose to but don't let your school become a cult.

- Just be a teacher, humbly sharing what you have gathered from long years of study and practice so that others can penetrate these mysteries for themselves.

A school should exist not only to teach but also to investigate, not only to formulate prematurely a finalized system but to remain creative, to go on testing theories by applying them and by validating ideas by experience."

Dr. Paul Brunton

The Art of Teaching Tai Chi

So far in this volume, in seven steps, we have considered the basic tools of the craft of teaching Tai Chi as a foundation that can help you to get started as a teacher.

Many of these tools apply to the teaching of any subject. However, in the same way that Tai Chi is more than a simple physical exercise system, teaching is more than just a craft that anyone can learn by following a set of instructions; it involves vast amounts of ingenuity, flexibility, creativity and perhaps even artistry.

As we have mentioned many times, every student is different and so our approach has to change and adapt to the needs of individuals in every class we teach. At the same time, our own Tai Chi skills and knowledge will continue to develop and evolve as we pass them on to others. We ourselves are still evolving as teachers after more than three decades of teaching.

Teaching Tai Chi is not a one-way street in which we repeat the same stuff, year after year, to various groups of people; it is a dynamic, interactive process that takes place between teachers and students: a mutual exploration of the boundless depths of Tai Chi Chuan that can benefit everyone and maybe contribute to the evolution of the art of Tai Chi Chuan itself. So let's consider how this works.

- If any student is having difficulty with a movement, you can investigate where that difficulty is coming from and so learn more about individual capabilities and the importance of subtle differences in posture and timing. On one occasion, many years ago, a gentleman was convinced that he had a congenital hip deformity which prevented him from turning to the left without throwing his body sideways and coming to rest in an uncomfortable and unstable position. Careful investigation revealed that he was simply turning his left foot outwards without turning his waist. Once he got the timing right, the problem disappeared and we gained a valuable insight that has helped many other students to avoid this error since then. As a teacher you can be moving so naturally that there are principles of timing that happen instinctively in your own body and it is not until you see other people struggling that you realise that not everyone finds such subtleties obvious.

- If you are interested in the martial aspects, you may have a group of like-minded students who are happy to work with you to discover which applications actually work in practice.

- If you are teaching forms, instead of simply showing and telling your students what to do, you can devise occasional experiments to allow them to discover and feel for themselves the qualities and principles that you are attempting to communicate.

In the final section of this book, at the request of one of our own students who is now an experienced instructor, we have shared with you some of the occasional activities that we have used in our own classes to support the more usual practice of learning the movements of a sequence. Our students have found these to be particularly helpful in deepening their understanding and enriching their experience of Tai Chi.

We have also included a section that gives further information on the levels of Tai Chi teaching and learning, in the hope that this might be useful to you when you are an experienced teacher and you have students who have been with you long enough to be considering teaching on their own.

With the inclusion of this chapter, we hope that this book will not only help you to launch your career as a teacher but will also be a useful handbook that you can refer to many times during the coming years.

Enrichment Exercises for Tai Chi Teachers

As well as the usual form instruction, push hands exercises and martial applications that are regularly practiced in Tai Chi classes, there are a whole host of occasional practical exercises that can help to enrich the learning experience for your students. Part of the art of teaching is to use your own imagination to find creative ways to help people to enjoy your lessons, overcome obstacles and deepen their understanding of the principles.

The following activities are the ones that we have used most often in our own classes. They include some that have been explained in detail in our previous books, such as those for learning how to breathe properly and how to use the waist. For these activities, a brief summary is offered, together with a note of where to go to find further explanations or more detailed instructions if you need them. We may also suggest extension work to allow you to explore some aspects more deeply.

For completeness, some activities are included that may seem pretty obvious or be things that your own teacher has used with you many times in class, such as the basic finger sensitivity exercise or the penny on the hand warm-up exercise.

We have also included several activities that we have created ourselves and do not appear elsewhere in our previous works, such as the healing qigong exercise and the 7 forms exercise, which our students have found to be especially valuable in enhancing their experience of Tai Chi and their appreciation of life in general.

Practitioners with an interest in the more 'spiritual' aspects of Tai Chi might find these exercises helpful, together with our sections on meditation, mindfulness and the spontaneous state.

For each activity, we look at how to do it and why we think it may be useful to you and your students, and point out any safety considerations, where appropriate.

We hope that this list will be a helpful resource that you can refer to whenever you need a boost to inspire you and get the creative juices flowing!

How to Sit Down Without Bending Your Knees

How? Invite your students, perhaps in their first lesson, to discover the difference between deliberately bending their knees - which tenses the knee joint and tends to tip them forward and make their bottom stick out behind them as if they were doing a squat - and imagining standing with their back against a wall and sliding down it until they are sitting on a ledge at a comfortable height with their back and head still upright and no undue tension in the sinews around their knees.

Why? As well as being safer and more comfortable for them to practice their Tai Chi in this way, it allows them to suspend the Crown Point, free up the waist, breathe properly and use the dantien effectively, as described in all of our previous books.

Breathing Exercises

How? Take your students through the breathing exercises for which detailed instructions are provided in Volume 1 of this series: *How to Move Towards Tai Chi Mastery*, Step 2.

In a horse-riding stance, let them try upper chest breathing, abdominal (Buddhist) breathing and dantien breathing (Taoist of Reverse breathing). Include the singing exercises so that they can experience the difference in the power available and how the sound is connected with the muscles of the abdomen. Make sure that they are very clear about the dantien breathing by the end of the session so they never imagine it to be simply the opposite of abdominal breathing.

Once they can do this properly, let them focus on this in their Tai Chi forms, which are likely to become more powerful as a result.

Why? Proper breathing is an essential requirement of all Tai Chi, if students are to gain the maximum benefits in terms of their health and the development of their internal power. Wrong advice can result in injury so it is very important that they know how to breathe correctly, especially when issuing Fa jin.

Safety note: Don't let your students push out the whole abdomen on the out breath, which could cause umbilical hernia. Avoid excessive 'tucking under' of the buttocks; just gently dropping the tailbone towards the floor is sufficient. Ask them to gently squeeze the pelvic floor muscles on the out breath and direct the force forwards and upwards rather than exerting downward pressure on the pelvic floor.

How to Uproot a Wall

How? If you have a suitable expanse of (strong, not plasterboard or wood) wall available, ask your students to line up along it and stand facing the wall in a forward shoulder-width stance with the toes of their front foot touching the wall and then ask them to place their hands on the wall in front of their chests. Ask them to push on the wall a) while breathing in, b) while breathing out and c) while breathing out using dantien breathing and keeping the back knee flexed. Ask them how it feels each time.

Why? This exercise allows them to discover how much power is available in Tai Chi and how to access it. (a) should feel as if they are trying to suck the wall towards them, (b) allows a better push, though still quite weak, but (c) will feel as if they are lifting the wall upwards from its foundations.

Where to find more information: 'How to Uproot a Wall' in *Your Tai Chi Companion Part 2* – Pages 19-20, and in *How to Move Towards Tai Chi Mastery*, Step 1, in a section called 'The Power of Dantien Breathing'.

Experiments with the Waist

How? Take your students through the exercises that allow them to feel and free up the waist, as described in detail in Volume 1: *How to Move Towards Tai Chi Mastery*, Step 2. The following is a further exploration of connectedness involving metaphors that were not included in that volume.

In a deep horse-riding stance, so that the hips cannot move, rest the arms on an imaginary cushion of air and then let the waist (side abdominal muscles) turn from side to side, with the arms trailing loosely behind on the imaginary cushion of air. Use metaphors as a basis for this exercise. Three useful metaphors are:

Pondweed - Imagine that the body is the stalk of a water-based plant and your arms are its fronds. As the stem twists, the fronds trail in the water.

The flag on a pole - Imagine that the body is a flagpole and the arms are a flag. As the pole rotates, the flag trails behind.

The spacewalk and the stone on a string - Imagine being a spaceman, floating in space while holding a piece of string to which a stone is attached. Throw the stone and see how it keeps going until the string becomes taut and pulls it back.

The important thing in all of these analogies is that the frond of pondweed, the flag and the stone on a string in space only move when they are dragged along. They have no independent movement. Once they start to move, they keep on going in that direction until they are dragged back. In the case of the arms, once the waist turns to the left, the arms start to follow to the left and the hands are pulled along behind. When the waist reaches its limit and flows back the other way, the arms don't know that yet so they continue on to the left until they feel the tug to the right from the waist, at which point they start to follow to the right.

Why? This exercise is designed to allow students to feel the connectedness between the waist, arms and fingers and gain a better understanding of one of the most important principles of Tai Chi, as described in the Tai Chi Classics: movements are directed by the waist and expressed through the arms, hands and fingers.

Where to find more detailed instructions: *How to Move Towards Tai Chi Mastery*, Step 2.

Experiments with the Dragon Body

How? Let the students move around the room taking on the characteristics of a bear, a tiger, snake, a bird and a dragon, in turn.

Why? Being a saggy, baggy bear on its hind legs encourages sinking and rooting. Walking like a tiger encourages smooth, powerful, controlled movements. Imagining a snake coiled in a horizontal figure of 8 or infinity loop around the midriff area encourages the correct use of the waist. Imagining the arms as snakes encourages the spiralling, drilling actions that can allow an arm to escape from an attempted grip while simultaneously striking an opponent, as well as increasing the overall fluidity of the form. Hands and fingers as light as the wing-tip feathers of a bird allows greater sensitivity (ting jin). Putting all of that together helps to develop the 'dragon body' and a freedom to move anywhere at will.

Where to find more detailed instructions: *How to Move Towards Tai Chi Mastery*, Step 3.

Put the Snake in the Box

How? Do any of the upper body movements of any Tai Chi sequence, or part thereof, while standing in a horse-riding stance. Then do it again inside an imaginary telephone kiosk, which restricts the arm movements so that they are unable to move more than a couple of inches to either side and prevents the waist from turning freely. Then imagine the glass shattering, allowing you to break free so that the waist and arms can now move and express your internal power fully.

Why? This exercise allows the students to feel the power of the dantien and waist as it is contained and then released. In traditional Wu Hao style Tai Chi, the movements are very small and compact, allowing vast amounts of internal power to be cultivated and stored rather than expressed.

Where to find more detailed instructions: *How to Move Towards Tai Chi Mastery*, Step 3.

The Finger Sensitivity Exercise

How? Working with a partner, students take turns to lead each other round the room by touching just the tip of their partner's index finger. To begin with, the leader's eyes are open and the follower's eyes are closed. Then repeat with both partners having their eyes open. Ask the students what they learned at each stage.

Why? Students may experience a degree of trust in each other and a sense of responsibility towards each other. They may discover that they have more sensory information available to them than they normally realise and that the exercise becomes more difficult when they have their eyes open. Sight is the dominant sense and very much linked to the thinking mind, so with eyes open they may find themselves trying to predict where their partner is going. They may even find themselves taking over the leading role instead of just listening, feeling and going where they are led. The usefulness of this exercise is that it leads to enhanced sensitivity and awareness (Ting Jin) in push hands and combat.

Extension work: If time allows, they may practice the eyes-open exercise three more times while changing the focus of their gaze each time, as follows:

1. Let them look around the room as they follow, but not at the partner who is leading them.

2. Both partners look into each other's eyes.

3. Let them rest their gaze lightly on their partner's upper chest area while opening up their peripheral awareness and being aware of everything in the room, including their partner.

Why? Looking around the room means that they will be distracted and not paying attention to what is happening with their partner. Looking into someone's eyes can be very intimidating for most people and it is how prize fighters try to 'psych each other out' by fixing them with a menacing gaze before a bout. Avoiding the eyes and resting the gaze calmly on the upper chest allows an overall awareness of one's opponent and peripheral surroundings without being caught up in the trance like state or general discomfort that eye-to eye contact can induce. This is a very useful insight for students going on to practice push hands or combat, in class and in competitions, and it could also be a useful habit if they ever needed to defend themselves in their everyday lives.

Further extension work: Students may repeat the exercise once more while both partners keep their eyes closed.

Why? When both partners have their eyes closed, the leader needs to be aware of everything in the room, without the benefit of sight, to avoid collisions and lead their partner safely. This calls for real focus on the present moment and close attention to sensory information, especially sound.

Safety note: When students have their eyes closed, the teacher needs to pay close attention to where they are going, to avoid accidental collisions, though this has rarely been a problem in practice, even in a very crowded room and even when both partners have their eyes closed, unless the students are busy chatting to each other rather than paying attention to what they are doing.

Where to find more information: *Your Tai Chi Companion Part 2* pp 34-40, and *How to Move Towards Tai Chi Mastery*, Step 7 in the section on Ting Jin

The Thumbs Experiment

How? Ask students to hold a hand out in front of them, palm down, as if resting their arm and hand on a cushion. Let the thumb relax and sink into the 'cushion' then bring it up level with the hand and ask where they can notice any new tension in the body.

Why? This exercise increases awareness of how a small amount of tension anywhere in the body, such as the amount required to lift a thumb, can affect the whole body and break the connectedness so that arms, backs and legs stiffen and lose their flexible resilience.

Where to find more information (including pictures): 'All Fingers and Thumbs' in Your Tai Chi Companion Part 2, Page 29.

Stationary Postures

How? Take any posture from any Tai Chi sequence and hold it still for several minutes. One of our own teachers used to make us do this for ten to twenty minutes at a time but it's one of those things that gets easier with practice and very much depends on the age, condition and capabilities of your students, so half a minute may be more than enough for some people. One of us used to do this for over an hour a day for over six months.

Why? To avoid discomfort, the body naturally sinks into its most upright, stable and comfortable position. Leaning forward or over-bending the knees can cause back pain, for example, so the student will naturally assume a more upright posture and drop their tailbone to relieve this. The posture then becomes self-correcting and the student takes a step towards becoming their own master. Longer periods of practice may help to develop inner strength, reduce unnecessary tension and cultivate a calm, focussed, peaceful mind.

Repetition of One Movement

How? Take any movement of the form and do it over and over again, either while standing still or while walking across the room.

Why? This is standard practice for most Tai Chi teachers and most classes probably include these repeated movements as a means of perfecting each one before progressing to the next or as a means of illustrating a particular teaching point. Some sequences already include such stretches of repetition, for example Part Wild Horse's Mane, Brush Knee and Push, Repulse Monkeys and Wave Hands in Clouds are often repeated three or more times in the forms of many styles.

Repetition of a Section

How? Repeat a small section, such as Ward Off, Roll Back, Press and Push, or the last section of the Beijing 24 step form, many times over in both directions as a kind of mini sequence or drill that is an entity in itself.

Why? Again, this is standard practice when teaching Tai Chi. Students can gain a lot from it as they don't have to worry about remembering a long sequence but can just focus on those few moments until they become natural and flowing. It might be worth mentioning that if they practice in their garden they may end up with a bald patch on their lawn.

The Penny on the Hand Exercise

This exercise is included because it is very popular with many instructors and their students and we have come across it in many classes and workshops we have attended.

Proceed with caution, however, as if it is done wrongly it can cause problems. If in any doubt, don't do it.

How? In a horse-riding stance, let your students place a coin on the palm of their hand. Or they can imagine a glass of water or a plate of spaghetti resting there. Bring the hand inwards so that the fingers point towards the waist, still with the palm upwards, and let it flow backwards and around in a large spiral, passing over the top of the head until it returns to its original position. It is easier to do this if they sink their weight down into their legs and let the waist turn freely as they go, rather than standing still and just using the arm. If they can do this exercise easily, they can try it with the other hand and then with both hands alternating continuously.

Why? When done safely, this exercise is great for increasing flexibility and co-ordination and discovering whole-body connectedness, as preparation for silk-reeling and the fluidity of the Tai Chi forms.

A word about safety. Explain that it is very important to do this slowly and keep the shoulders relaxed throughout. Let them pay full attention to how their own body is feeling. Do not overstrain any joint by forcing it to move in an unnatural way in an effort to keep the hand horizontal. If you, or they, drop the coin, it doesn't matter. (Best not to try it with Spaghetti Bolognese until you are very proficient!). If they feel any pulling or discomfort, they should stop. Extra care should be taken with older students or anyone with arthritis or other joint problems and some may not be able to do it at all, especially if they have a frozen shoulder or rotator cuff syndrome. If a student does not want to do this exercise, for whatever reason, don't ask them to.

Silk-reeling

How? Exercises that encourage what the classics refer to as 'the delicate reeling-in of silk', include holding the hands out in front of you and rotating the wrists so that the hands move inwards, as if beckoning to someone, or outwards, as if pushing them away. You can make the circles smaller or larger so that the hands pass by your waist and come behind you before returning to their original position. Allowing the knees to flex and sinking down as the hands move towards the body makes this an excellent form of exercise which builds strength and flexibility. Doing the breast stroke is very similar to the outward circling one. Other exercises that involve types of silk reeling include drawing circles with the arms, as in Lazy Tying Coat, and Cloud Hands.

Essential requirements of any silk reeling exercises include sinking down, using the waist and dantien and dropping the shoulders or keeping the 'lead cape' on (see below). An important point is that the students can learn the difference between:

• allowing the movement to come from the hand and wrist and be transmitted throughout the rest of the body and

• allowing it to start in the dantien and be transmitted via the waist and arms into the fingers, as described in the Tai Chi Classics.

Why? These exercises improve flexibility and promote the development of whole-body connectedness. This principle is fundamental to all of Tai Chi but is most obvious in Chen Style. Chen Style teachers may use lots of different silk-reeling exercises but practitioners of all styles can benefit from them. There are many different ones and each school may have its own favourites. The following are examples of our own.

How to Swing an Axe

How? Ask your students to perform the action of hammering a nail into a piece of wood and give their full attention to which muscles they use for that. Then ask them to imagine swinging and axe to chop down a tree and again feel the muscles involved.

Why? This exercise should illustrate what we mean by whole-body power and how it differs from simple arm strength. Ask them to use the axe-swinging muscles as they move through their Tai Chi form.

Pulling the Boat In

How? In a deep horse-riding stance that does not allow the hips to move, and without leaning forwards, imagine standing next to a lake and using a rope to pull in a boat that is some distance in front of you, hand over hand, towards your dantien. Use your whole body, allowing your waist to turn freely, each hand pulling inwards to the dantien and then around past your waist, as in the penny on the hand exercise, and stretching out along the rope as far as possible before pulling in again.

Why? Like 'swinging an axe', this exercise can help students to make a huge breakthrough in experiencing whole-body connectivity. From this movement, they can progress to issuing fa jing in a 'cannon fist'.

Drilling

How? There are various types of drilling. You can try the following experiments.

1. Start with the hand beside the waist with the palm upwards and then move it forwards into a push position, using a spiralling action.

2. With the palm down to begin with, let your arm and hand spiral forwards like a snake coiling around a branch of a tree until the palm is upwards and about level with your shoulder.

The only real difference between the above two exercises is that the hand and arm rotate clockwise or counter-clockwise. In reality, the arms may wriggle and writhe continuously, so that your opponent is unable to either grab you or to escape your strikes.

Why? Quite apart from its benefits in improving the flexibility of the wrist and fingers, drilling is a very valuable martial technique. It is a coiling, snaking, corkscrew-like motion that can allow you to wriggle free from an attempt to grab your arm and perhaps also to use that same arm to strike your opponent with finger tips, palm or fist. The fingers or fist can continue to twist as they reach their target while a palm strike can be delivered with Fa Jin explosive power. With practice, drilling can become very quick and powerful, like a snake spitting poison.

Where to find more information: *How to Use Tai Chi for Self-defence*, Step 4.

The Lead Cape Experiments

How? Two very useful experiments are:

1. Let your students hold out an arm in front of them or to the side and then experience the difference between dropping an arm by just lowering their hand and then dropping it again by imagining a heavy weight on their arm above the elbow. They can test this with a partner who allows them to press on an arm while resisting their downward pressure. This movement is similar to cracking a whip and it can be seen in most styles as a potential use of an arm during Single Whip while the other arm forms the hook or 'crane's beak'. It can also be experienced in some versions of Cloud Hands, Lazy Tying Coat and some silk-reeling exercises.

2. If a punch bag is available, let them push the bag with their shoulder and elbow high and then again with their elbow dropped and a feeling of weight applied to their upper arm, like a lead cape draped around their shoulders or a medicine ball strapped to their upper arm. Let them discover which is the most powerful and where that power is coming from.

Why? This is often the moment where a student makes a quantum leap from intermediate to advanced level as they really begin to feel their internal power. Considerable downward pressure can be exerted during experiment 1 and tremendous forwards and upwards power is available for palm strikes and pushes in experiment 2.

Safety note: When working with a partner, make sure the partner is expecting the downward force and do this exercise slowly, without any sudden jerking that could, potentially, injure the partner's shoulder.

In any exercises involving partner work, students should have martial arts licences (member to member insurance) and should practice carefully and with due respect for each other's safety. All such activities should be closely supervised at all times.

Where to find more information: *How to Move Towards Tai Chi Mastery*, Step 4.

The See-saw Experiments

How? Ask your students to explore the way that a downward pressure on the upper arm causes an upward movement of the wrist, as they lift their hands in Heaven and Earth, for example. They can test this with a partner. One person tries to lift a hand in front of them while the other places a hand on their forearm and tries to prevent the upward movement. Then the exercise is repeated but, instead of focussing on lifting the hand, the focus is on a downward force above the elbow that causes the forearm to rise and is difficult for the partner to resist.

Why? As it says in the Tai Chi Classics: "For every up, there is also down". You don't have to take a see-saw off its moorings and lift the whole thing in the air to make one end of it move upwards, you just press down on the opposite end. This is an excellent exercise for developing peng jing.

Where to find more information: *How to Move Towards Tai Chi Mastery*, Step 4.

Peng Jing Exercises

How? Use metaphors to help your students to experience the feeling of ward-off energy or peng jin (or jing) throughout their bodies. For example, they can imagine being as bouncy as a rubber ball, or folding and unfolding like an accordion as they practice press and push, or they can imagine loading the 'five bows' on the yin movements of their form and then releasing their power in their yang movements. They may also imagine a balloon expanding in their arms or water filling their limbs like a pressure hose or their arms filling with vitality like live snakes.

Why? Peng jin is one of the most important qualities for the effectiveness of Tai Chi as a martial art. Even for those students with no interest in the fighting aspects, it may allow them to develop a kind of pliancy and resilience that helps them to release stress and perhaps become less prone to injury from falls.

Where to find more information: *How to Move Towards Tai Chi Mastery*, Step 4, and *How to Use Tai Chi for Self-defence*, Step 3 .

Exploring Prime, Coil Release

How? Let the students feel the slow build-up of peng jin in an arm and then release it, paying close attention to the process. They then repeat it while a partner lightly touches their arm and compares it with a fully relaxed arm and a stiff, tense arm.

Why? Being able to sense your opponent's intention to strike before they actually release their force is a valuable skill. As it says in the classics: "My opponent moves a little; I move first".

Where to find more information: *How to Use Tai Chi for Self-defence*, Step 3.

Explore Yin and Yang

How? Ideally, explore yin and yang in all the movements and applications you teach. However, a particularly useful movement to explore is the brush knee push exercise (sometimes called brush knee and twist step). Simply stand still in a forward, shoulder-width stance and let the front hand perform a circular, beckoning movement while the other comes around in a larger circle to perform a Tai Chi push. Turn the waist and let the weight sink from the front leg to the back leg as you yield and into the front leg as you strike and just keep repeating this over and over until the students can notice the alternating yielding and attacking, upward palm and downward palm, breathing in and breathing out, yin and yang. Do the same with the other leg forward, for balance.

Why? The concept of yin and yang is fundamental to Tai Chi and indeed to all life and the workings of the universe in general. The above exercise helps to illustrate this. It was used by our teacher, Dr. Zhu Guang, in answer to the question: "How can Tai Chi be summed up, in a nutshell?"

Where to find more information: *How to Use Tai Chi for Self-defence*, Step 2.

Practice the Form with Martial Intent

How? Just go through the form while imagining oneself to be on a battlefield, using the movements to fend off multiple assailants as you go.

Why? This is not just because some students may be interested in the fighting aspects of their martial art but also because even those who are only there for the health and spiritual aspects can benefit from this exercise. By visualising the applications of the movements, they are likely to perform them more accurately and so gain the maximum health benefits from them.

The 'Cricket Spin-bowler' or 'Galaxy' Exercise

How? Circle both arms in the same direction, with the shoulders and elbows dropped and each elbow as the centre of a circle, one hand following the other as if throwing a ball by the over-arm method. The shape this makes in the air is reminiscent of the Tai Chi symbol and can be seen illustrated by graphics during the movements of (dare we say it?) 'water benders' in the film *The Last Airbender*, and in many of the connecting movements of the 48 step Taiji sequence. The movement is also reminiscent of the two arms of a spiral galaxy turning in space. This movement may also be known as 'threading' since one hand threads over the other arm before circling.

Why? As well as providing a very fluid link between one movement and another during a sequence, this is an extremely useful manoeuvre if someone has their hands around your throat, allowing you to deflect, wrap and control their arms while bringing one hand around again to strike them or knock them over. The more this is practiced, the more it becomes a natural reflex that can happen very fast if needed.

Where to find more information: *How to Use Tai Chi for Self-defence*, Step 4 under 'wrapping'.

The Shape of the Form

How? Ask students to consider the foot-map of their form and the area of floor space required. This is best done while they are on holiday at the coast and can look at the footprints they leave in wet sand after doing their form correctly.

Why? Many students have no idea of how much space they need to practice their form or where to stand when they start. They may habitually stand too close to the back of the room to allow themselves to take wide enough stances, or find themselves having to step backwards so that they don't run into a wall half-way through the sequence. Although you can position your students where they need to be in class, it is better if they understand why, from having seen the foot map for themselves.

Practice Tai Chi in Water

How? If your students are swimmers and have access to a safe swimming pool, you might recommend to them that a great way for them to train is to stand in water that is chest deep at their full height or neck deep when they sink and root by allowing their knees to bend a little. They can then attempt to practice their forms very slowly without floating away. They can also practice any movements that allow them to release their fa jin, with their hands close to the surface of the water.

Why? Tai Chi is sometimes referred to as 'swimming in air'. Good swimmers are often naturally good at Tai Chi. Practicing Tai Chi (or any martial art) in water has many advantages. It takes the weight off the joints and allows free movement, high kicks and even flying side-kicks. It is a brilliant way to encourage rooting (it takes good stability to avoid drifting off in the water). Students can see how their arms naturally trail behind in the water as their waist turns. It also allows them to actually see the effectiveness of their fa jin as compared with ordinary percussive strikes. A normal push will make the water plop a little but a fa jin push will send a huge plume of water right across the pool.

Tactical Note: It's best to do this when there are not many other bathers around (to avoid nuisance, funny looks or potential litigation!)

In the past, one of us ran some very successful Aqua Tai Chi and Aqua King Fu classes. If you want to explore this option, you need to be a good swimmer, check that your students can swim and obtain any necessary qualification for teaching exercise safely in water, such as a life-saving award. An ideal pool for such classes would have a constant depth that allows all students to stand up and has no deep end.

Perform Tai Chi at Different Speeds

How? Go more slowly than normal or more quickly than normal. We normally teach Tai Chi forms at a medium kind of speed where the movements synchronise with an average breathing rate of about 12 breaths per minute and then we gradually slow it down to around 8 breaths per minute or less. When students know the movements well, we may gradually speed up and do it very quickly on some occasions.

Why? Students often get into the habit of always doing their forms at a particular speed, to the point where, if they see other people doing it more quickly or slowly, they insist they are doing it wrongly. However, by always practicing at the same speed, they can miss potential benefits.

Doing the forms slowly encourages precision, improves balance and allows more time to see what the teacher is doing. It also encourages deeper, slower breathing and becomes more meditative and mindful. Students are more likely to avoid bad habits such as incorrect footwork that can happen unconsciously when going too fast. As a teacher, it gives you more time to see what your students are doing. If people want to take more breaths during very slow forms, they are welcome to do so but slowing the breathing along with the movements is a learned skill and more breath control is gained with practice.

Doing the forms quickly helps students to get past the robotic stage so they start to flow and feel their internal power. It also allows them to become more familiar with the kind of speeds they would need to move at in a combat situation. Some styles have specific 'fast form' sequences. Some sequences, such as the Chen Style forms, naturally have slower or faster sections, depending on where the energy is contained or expressed. Always practicing at a constant rhythm and tempo could inhibit the development of internal power.

Safety note: Some students, especially older students, may find it more difficult to keep their balance when they attempt to move more slowly. They may hurry from one movement to the next before they have time to fall over. This may be because their footwork or timing is wrong but they usually go so fast that you don't have a chance to work out what they are doing. This exercise gives you an opportunity to notice and correct these errors, which could otherwise cause injuries further down the line. As our teacher, Dr. Zhu Guang, used to say, "If you always rush through the form, nothing of value can truly be learned at that speed." It is not always a question of poor balance, however. Some students may be suffering from arthritis or back problems which make it painful for them to have their weight in one leg for more than a second. The constant shifting of weight during a Tai Chi sequence of average speed may be fine for them but if they go very slowly, they may struggle with postures such as White Crane or kicks, where their weight is in one leg for a little too long for comfort.

Where to find more information: *Your Tai Chi Companion Part 2* pp 34-40 offers a more detailed account of the rationale behind working at different speeds.

The 7 Forms Exercise

This exercise takes about an hour to complete, depending on the length of the sequence used, and involves the students performing the same short sequence seven times. The first dozen or so movements, from any style, will do. Because the sequence required is quite short, students can have a go at this exercise after only a few weeks of study and gain benefits that can help them at an important stage of their learning, though they may wish to do it again later, when they are more experienced.

How? Give instructions of what to focus on each time they do their form, as follows:

1. Let them just do the form ***as they normally do it*** in class.

2. Then do it while ***focussing on their breathing***. Importantly, they should not try to do anything WITH the breathing, just notice what it does naturally as they move.

Afterwards, ask what they noticed. They will normally say that they found that they were breathing in during the yin movements and out on the yang movements. Let them try doing a push while breathing in to see what effect that has. They will notice that it feels unnatural, which means that they can trust the body to know when to breathe in and out, without interfering.

3. Ask the students to do their form again, this time ***with their eyes closed***. If anyone really can't tolerate moving with their eyes closed, perhaps because it makes them feel dizzy or insecure, ask if they would like to partially close their eyes so that they can see where they are going through their eyelashes while still remaining internally focussed.

Afterwards, ask them how they found that. They may have felt wobbly or unstable, which is good because they can then think about why that was. In most cases it is usually that their stances were too narrow or they were not sitting down into their stances or not using their waist. When the eyes are closed, these things are more easily noticed by the student, rather than having to be pointed out by the teacher. In this way, a student begins to become their own master.

4. Let the students spend a few minutes doing Shou Shi (or Sau Gong), inwards circling arm movements, while imagining gathering energy from the universe. Then, without touching anything, let them ***feel the energy in the palms of their hands*** (perhaps as warmth, coolness or tingling) and keep this awareness of the palms of their hands while moving through their Tai Chi form. They can imagine this energy streaming from their palms so that they can squash it, stretch it, trail it or whatever. For this exercise: keep the hands relaxed and don't touch anything: don't let the fingers touch the palm in punches or the hook of single whip, and don't let the hand touch the opposite wrist or arm in press or shoulder press.

As they come to rest, your students might like to use any residual energy to do the Healing Chi Exercise, which we will look at in a moment.

Afterwards, ask how that felt. Students often enjoy this exercise because it can feel as if there really is some kind of energy in their hands but if they don't feel anything, tell them that's perfectly fine. It's the visualisation that's important. Their forms are likely to become less robotic and more flowing after this exercise.

Then ask them to do their form three more times, as follows. Tell them not to overthink this, as the instructions may seem quite strange, a bit like a Zen koan. They can just do the best they can to follow the instruction.

5. ***Observing the space inside and outside the body***.

6. ***Observing how the movements shape the space***.

7. ***Observing how the space shapes the movements.***

At the end of the seven forms exercise, ask the following questions:

- If someone had been watching from outside of the room, would they have seen a group of people doing the same sequence seven times? (Students will usually agree).
- Internally, did they themselves feel the same on each of the seven occasions? (Students will usually say no).
- If they had different experiences, why was that?
- Would they agree that the experience changed, depending on where they were resting their attention?
- If the focus of our attention can change our experience, is that just in our Tai Chi forms, or is this a wider phenomenon? Is it possible that our focus of attention can change our experience of reality in our everyday lives? Ask for examples such as the attitude of gratitude instead of resentment, or focussing on strengths and goodness in ourselves and others instead of weakness.
- In this exercise, instructions were given on where to rest the attention. When they practice at home or in class, who normally decides where they focus their attention?

Interestingly, many students ask if they can do the bit where they focus on energy again sometimes. The answer, of course is yes, any time they choose!

Why? This exercise has been found by many students to be incredibly empowering as they realise their own ability to transform their lives by choosing where to rest their attention.

If time allows. You may want to share with them a little story that further illustrates this point.

A young man goes to see his master. He has with him a small notepad and a pencil and asks the master to please write down some instructions on how to become enlightened. The master takes the notepad and pencil, writes something for a few seconds, and then hands it back to the disciple. The young man is very disappointed to see that only one word has been written: "Attention." So he begs the master to add more. He needs clearer instructions, more information if he is ever to become enlightened. The master smiles and takes back the notepad, returning it to the student only a few seconds later. This time, it says: "ATTENTION! ATTENTION! ATTENTION!"

The Healing Chi Exercise

How? Start with a few minutes of Shou Shi (or Sau Gong), inwards circling arm movements, while imagining gathering energy from the universe. If you like, you can ask your students to feel a ball of energy about the size of a beach ball between their hands and try squashing it in, stretching it out and turning it over a few times, then draw it back into the dantien.

They can then close their eyes and you can ask them to lay their hands firmly on any part of their body that has been bothering them during the week, maybe a bad knee or an aching back or whatever. Ask them to feel the energy passing from their hands deep into that place, bringing ease and comfort, maybe as a warmth or a coolness or a tingling sensation. If no part of their body has been bothering them, ask them to just rest their hands on their lower abdomen.

After a minute or so, ask everyone to stand comfortably with their hands on their abdomen and imagine energy flowing from the dantien down into the bones of their legs and upwards into their spine, arms and head, until it is as if their entire skeleton is packed with brilliant light, healing and making everything new. Then let the healing light spread outwards beyond the surface of the skin, so that they seem to have a kind of glow about them from the top of the head right down to the tips of their fingers and toes and it feels as if every cell in their body has been washed clean and made new .

Then invite them to turn their palms outwards in front of their heart and send loving, healing energy out into the world, as if it is flowing through them like a tide. They can direct it to someone they know who needs some healing right now, or just to the world in general.

They can then open their eyes, bow to the Tao (entire cosmos) and thank the universe for its healing.

Why? Whatever you think about the idea of 'healing energy' and suchlike, our advice would be to give this a go. As a friend of ours once said to us, towards the end of her long career as a professional physiotherapist, when asked for her opinion about the efficacy of alternative practices such as osteopathy and chiropractic as compared with physiotherapy: "I have come to the conclusion that any therapy, if it's safe, can be equally effective. If a patient believes it will work, it probably will." As scientists (a physiologist and a biochemist), as well as Tai Chi teachers, we have come to appreciate the contribution made by the mind in promoting the healing process and how much our physical, mental, emotional and spiritual health can be influenced by our own beliefs and expectations. Our approach has always been to keep our feet on the floor and grounded in science, yet remain open-minded enough to recognise the benefits of phenomena whose existence has ample verification but for which science has yet to provide a fully satisfactory explanation. The placebo and nocebo effects would seem to us to fall into this category.

The Peripheral Awareness Exercise – Stepping Back

How? Ask students to place the palm of their hand in front of their face and study it very carefully. Then ask them to continue to rest their gaze lightly on the hand but open up their peripheral awareness to include everything around them, as wide as they can. Let them practice switching from 'tunnel vision' to wider awareness and back several times. Encourage your students to practice this skill regularly, in many different situations, and you will have done more to increase their chances of survival on the street that any number of martial skills you could teach them.

Why? This exercise encourages the habit of staying 'switched on' to their surroundings, which might make them less vulnerable to the distraction techniques used by criminals on the street. For those interested in meditation, it can be extended to include the habit of mentally 'stepping back' from the body, emotions and thoughts and simply being present in the moment and watching the movements of the mind or settling into the stillness of the quiet mind and opening the attention to the vast ocean of peace underlying everything.

Where to find more information: *How to Use Tai Chi for Self-defence*, First section of Step 7 for the technique and then all of Step 6 for context. For the meditative aspects, see 'Teach Meditation and Mindfulness' below.

Teach Meditation and Mindfulness

If you view Tai Chi as a type of moving meditation or a mindful practice, then the inclusion of a section on how to teach those aspects might seem unremarkable or even essential. On the other hand, if you see Tai Chi mainly as a method of self-defence, you might wonder what relevance this part of the book could possibly have for you. So in this section we will take a look at the various ways in which an understanding of meditation can be useful, whichever angle you are coming from.

Tai Chi is widely known as a type of moving meditation and therefore, as a Tai Chi teacher, people will expect you to know a lot about it. So let's start with a clear definition of what we mean by 'meditation' and 'mindfulness'.

What is Mindfulness?

Being mindful is simply being fully awake and aware in the present moment. It's very, very simple yet, for most of us, it can take quite a bit of practice at first as the natural state of things is to get so caught up in our own thoughts that we barely notice what is happening around us a lot of the time. Just by bringing our attention back to the present moment, we can disengage from all the usual clutter that goes on in our heads - mostly thoughts about stuff that has happened in the past or might happen in the future – and instead find rest in simply noticing the now.

The benefits of this range from a deeper appreciation of our surroundings and the people we are with, to relief from the common and sometimes destructive habits of analysing, judging and perhaps even criticising everything, including our own thoughts and feelings. As a Tai Chi teacher, you will naturally find yourself encouraging mindfulness.

How? Tai Chi itself is a type of mindful practice since, when you perform any Tai Chi sequence, your attention is in the now. By its nature, Tai Chi is a complex discipline to learn, so your students will normally be very focused on what they are doing rather than on what is going on outside the building or in their lives generally. Once they know a sequence well, you can gradually encourage them to go from 'doing' mode to 'being' mode, i.e. experiencing and expressing the forms rather than trying to 'do them right' all the time.

Why? Teaching people this habit of being in the present moment sometimes, whether during Tai Chi or during a sitting meditation, or even while ironing a shirt or washing up, is a powerful way to help them to reduce stress, find contentment and generally improve their quality of life. It is a habit that can also come to their aid in a crisis and help them to remain calm while they do what needs to be done.

What is Meditation?

The state of meditation, in its purest sense, is simply being, with no thoughts at all in mind. To reach this state, we can use various meditation techniques to allow the mind to become still. So when we speak of meditation, we are normally including both the process and the goal.

In order to use any meditation technique, you need to be mindful of what is taking place in your own mind. So mindfulness, while not the same thing as meditation, is a prerequisite of meditation. If you were watching a drama on TV, you could, at any time, switch off and just look at the blank screen. Of course, this would presuppose that you were fully aware that you were watching TV and you had not become so immersed in the drama that you fully believed yourself to be one of the characters in it.

How? Teaching meditation does not require complex skills. Having a simple approach, such as sitting down for a few minutes and watching the breathing, is not only sufficient but actually preferable to anything more exotic. In fact, when faced with the challenge of leading a group in a seated meditation, one of our trainee instructors once said: "I'm not sure about all the best ways of doing meditation, so just close your eyes and breathe." So that's what we all did; and it was a great meditation!

Watching the breathing is a very natural method but there are many others to choose from. Whether you listen to the sound of a word or phrase (mantra) repeating in your mind, or watch a candle flame or just listen to the silence behind all the sounds, or move through the flowing sequence of your Tai Chi form, you are basically focussing your attention on just one thing, instead of all the usual clutter. Thoughts will inevitably appear from time to time, like pop-up menus on a computer screen. That doesn't mean that you are somehow not very 'good at' meditation, it just means that you have noticed a natural process of the human mind and you then have the power to choose what to do next, whether to lose yourself in the thought for a while or simply to return your attention to the breathing (or mantra or whatever) for a while longer. Like most skills, that gets easier with practice.

Why? Meditation is a kind of mental downtime where you remind yourself that you are not just a body playing a role in the drama of life, with all the thoughts, emotions, opinions and beliefs that go along with that. Instead you can watch that passing show, as if from a distance, and let it go for a while so that you can rest in the profound peace underlying everything and 'recharge your batteries' before diving in and participating again. As a bonus, you will then be more likely to participate in a more mindful and internally peaceful way, rather than being tossed around in the emotional turmoil of everyday life. This may even lead to what is often referred to as 'spiritual enlightenment' or a truer perception of reality..

Meditation and Martial Arts

You don't need to learn to meditate if you just want to learn how to fight, but a martial art is about learning self-protection skills so that you don't need to fight in the first place. It's about self-mastery: learning how your own mind works and how to use it effectively. In a fight, it's essential to avoid 'losing it' through fear or anger or even a desire to 'be the best' or 'kick ass'. It's also important not to become distracted or paralysed into inactivity.

Out on the street, we might be able to lessen the risk of violent conflict by staying 'switched on' and 'mindful' of our surroundings. The habit of stepping back and taking a wider view also helps us to avoid trance states induced by others. In a trance state, people are more open to suggestion and anyone who knows this - such as stage hypnotists, salespeople, magicians, the media, the advertising industry and politicians - can use it to further their own interests The opposite of a trance state is to be fully present in the moment, take a wider view and choose where to focus your attention.

By calming down and lowering the emotional temperature, we access the higher cortex and are able to look at things more objectively. As we step back further into the observing self and let go of the need to work things out, do things and fix things, we can just be present in the moment and see even more clearly what needs to be done. This can allow us to be in a state of flow, in which the mind and body work perfectly, whether we are creating a work of art, performing a Tai Chi sequence or neutralizing the movements of an opponent.

Any physical technique is only useful if the person's mental state allows them to use it or, better still, avoid having to use it at all, so passing on the ability to maintain an awake, aware and quiet mind is possibly more important than any number of secret techniques you might have in your repertoire.

Explore the Spontaneous State

How? Ask your students to find a way to connect any two Tai Chi movements that don't normally follow each other in any of their usual forms. Then ask them to add another movement… and another… until they are moving spontaneously in any direction they choose around the room. Don't do it with them or they may find themselves copying you, but don't watch them too closely at first or you could make them feel overly self-conscious and embarrassed.

Why? Quite apart from the need for spontaneity in combat, there are deeper practical and philosophical considerations. After they have had a little practice and overcome any initial reluctance or self-consciousness, you will probably find that your students are now inventing new, unique transition movements as they go, yet they are still following the Tai Chi principles, so their invented sequences are still recognisable as Tai Chi. If they have reached a high level with their usual forms, they will probably discover that these new movements are being driven by the spiralling of the waist, in response to their conscious intention to move in each new direction.

This is the spontaneous state, for which prescribed forms can be seen as preparation. When your students begin to go spontaneous, they can flow wherever they choose yet be aware of the momentum of the underlying process and at this stage it may be worth reflecting on the following analogies, which can lead to a deeper understanding of Tai Chi and also of life in general.

The Car Analogy

When you drive a car, you are in control, yet the car has its own momentum. Once it has started to move, you can consciously slow down, speed up or change direction, yet the overall fluidity of motion at any instant has to take account of what went before it.

It's the same with the Tai Chi form. Driven by your will, it also has its own momentum. Once it starts to flow, you can speed up, slow down, flow in new directions, using the waist like the steering wheel. The movement at each instant is a continuation of what went before, powered by the engine of the dantien, fuelled by the energy of the universe and overseen by the conscious self which observes and directs the whole process.

Transitions

In many Tai Chi forms, some movements, such as Cloud Hands, are repeated three or more times. We can even practice these repeating bits as an exercise in themselves, over and over again, until we feel really comfortable with them, and when we really master them we can learn a lot from them in terms of underlying principles and ways of moving. But sooner or later, we have to get from one familiar bit to another: we have to make a transition.

These are the complicated bits - there is no set pattern to follow and many students struggle with them at first - but they still follow the Tai Chi principles and they have a grace, fluidity and logical process of their own.

In the spontaneous state, when the Tai Chi principles have been fully internalised, transitions tend to arise quite naturally, without too much interference from the rational brain. Each may be a unique way of moving from one position another but, by following the internal principles, we are still doing Tai Chi. In fact it could be said that we are experiencing Tai Chi in its purest sense: participating in the process of creation; Yin and Yang emerging from the stillness of Wu Chi, interchanging continuously and then returning to the source.

Tai Chi as a Metaphor for Life

Tai Chi transitions and the principles underlying them have wider implications. Life itself is a creative process. In our own journey through life, there may be periods where everything stays relatively settled and we have a feeling that we are more or less in control, maybe even a bit bored sometimes, but eventually along comes period of transition.

Change is inevitable and often unplanned. Trying to hold onto things exactly as they are is a sure way to end up frustrated and stressed. When we are going through a period of change, we can sometimes do it through our own conscious choice and feel relatively in control, but at other times the whole thing comes at us out of the blue and we can feel that the ground has dropped out from under our feet. We may feel quite lost for a while until we regain our bearings.

But when we look back at these links in the chain, we may see that they were often the times that made us stronger or wiser, the ones that made the greatest contributions to our growth, just as the transitions in the Tai Chi form are not just there to tie the good bits together, they are potentially the bits that can teach us the most about what Tai Chi is really about.

Transitions are not just random movements; they obey the Tai Chi principles. You can trust these principles and also trust yourself as you flow through them seamlessly - just as you can in life. You learn the principles during the quiet times, the orderly times. Then, when the going gets tough, you can trust yourself and your principles (like honesty, integrity and compassion) to help you through and keep you afloat until you reach the quieter waters up ahead.

There's no need to detach yourself from everything, which would be a bit like trying to get out of your car while it's still moving; you can remain in control and direct the movements while maintaining an overall wide perspective as you go with the flow.

The Wave Analogy

In Tai Chi, once we begin to move, there's no stopping and starting or hesitation until we finally bring the whole thing to its close and return to Wu Chi - perfect stillness that contains the potential for everything. In motion, Tai Chi is like a great river, with waters that we can store or release at will, or like a great wave crossing a boundless sea.

A wave is transient, its molecules are changing continuously, yet it somehow preserves its identity as a wave and we can feel the relentless power and momentum of the surge and continue to flow with it.

Our lives are fluid and continuous, just like the Tai Chi form, and although we have free will, conscious choice and the power of intention, which allows us to speed up, slow down, change direction and attract to us those things to which we pay the most attention, we still go forward with the momentum of the flow.

Once we truly understand and feel at one with this flow, we can transform it in a creative, yet co-operative, way and achieve not only our own individual potential but also the potential of the wave and the potential of the ocean it emerges from, which is our true identity.

As both scientists and sages have come to realise, we are not small, mechanical objects, surviving in, and separate from, an uncaring universe; we are living expressions of that universe, just as a wave is an expression of the ocean. In the spontaneous Tai Chi state, we can move with the wave and be the ocean.

The Tai Chi Principles as a Rap Poem

To help your students to remember the Tai Chi principles, you could invite them to learn our Tai Chi Rap poem:

The Tai Chi Rap

Back:
Keep it straight, and relax.
Head:
In a line with your back.
Knees:
Keep them soft, sink down.
Feet:
Keep them rooted to the ground.

Let your waist keep turning
Like the coiling of a snake;
Let your hands be as light as if
You're floating in a lake;
Keep your shoulders down and level,
Keep your elbows low
Like a puppet with no strings attached
To shoulder or elbow.

Yield
To an incoming attack,
Take it round in a circle
Spit it out, give it back.
Crouching low like a tiger
That's preparing for a leap,

You can rise up like a dragon
That's been woken from its sleep.

Be aware of all directions
While your mind rests in the void
And keep your sense of humour
So you never get annoyed.
Stepping back from thoughts and feelings,
Keep it real, keep it cool.
Be aware of the connections
Of the drops within the pool.

Keep the whole thing moving
And keep going with the flow
Without doing any doing,
Without knowing what you know.
When your mind is as calm
And as vast as the sea,
Using power from your centre,
You'll be doing Tai Chi.

g Hamilton

Levels of Teaching and Learning

If you are new to teaching, the idea that some of your students will one day be in the position that you are in now may seem to be a very long way off but, if you persevere, it is almost inevitable that some of them will stay with you to the point where they are ready to take on students of their own.

So, for completeness and to make this handbook a valuable resource that you can refer to many times over the years, we will say something here about what to do when your students reach this stage.

As we mentioned previously in Step 4, in our own school, the levels of skill that people pass through on their Tai Chi journey can be summarised, in terms not merely of content but also of quality, as follows:

Level 1 – The ability to perform a short Tai Chi sequence all the way through, obeying very basic principles so that what they are doing is recognisable as Tai Chi. They have a go at some pushing hands and sword drills but their skills are very rudimentary at this stage. On average, it normally takes about a year for a student to reach this point.

Level 2 – After at least another two years of training, often a lot more, depending on the student and how regularly they attend, they may reach level 2, which includes the ability to perform one long sequence such as the Yang Long Form or two shorter forms such as the Beijing 24 step form, plus a weapons form, to a good standard in that it is structurally correct and follows all the basic principles of Tai Chi. At this point, they must also be able to demonstrate the martial applications of some of the main movements of their forms, such as Peng, Lu, Ji, An, and be able to participate in both fixed step and moving step push hands in a way that does not rely on external strength but is not floppy, unstable or lacking structure.

Level 3 – Achieving this level does not require the student to learn new forms, though they may wish to do so in order to explore various aspects of the principles more deeply. Instead, the student focusses on examining their existing forms and the underlying principles more thoroughly and developing their internal power. They reach level 3 when they are able to express their peng jin, or ward-off energy, throughout their body and their movements arise naturally from the waist and dantien. In partner work, they have developed a high level of sensitivity to the intentions of the opponent and can respond in an appropriate manner, using energy rather than force, where appropriate. They can apply a wide range of techniques from their forms successfully in a realistic bout of push hands and have some understanding of the main types of jing or jin.

There are higher levels than this! We will come back to these later.

When Might a Student be Ready to Teach?

In our own school:

Level 2 is the minimum required to be able to teach a Tai Chi sequence to others in a way that is unlikely to cause injury to the students.

Level 3 is the minimum required to be able to teach the full martial art, including push hands and applications, in a way that is effective.

At this level, the teacher would have a depth of understanding and skill that would enable him or her to recognise the level of development of their students, including the internal aspects.

Of course, not all students reaching Level 3 will wish to become teachers but they may continue to develop their skills to a higher level anyway. Conversely, there is a slight possibility that, once a person has permission to teach, they may 'rest on their laurels' and stop developing their skills, or even go backwards from that point. This is particularly likely if they gain teacher status too soon and have not yet reached the stage where they are able to use their own internal understanding as a guide and motivator for their future development.

When we issue our teaching certificate, we hope that the new instructor will use this as a starting point for their future journey towards mastery. We have found that most do, by continuing to develop their forms skills in our classes, by getting together in small groups to train their martial skills, by learning through the experience gained from teaching, and by travelling further afield to attend seminars by other teachers and gain a wider perspective of the art.

With regard to learning from other teachers, however, a word of caution is necessary here. Outside our school, we have met people who have spent years going along to an endless succession of seminars and workshops by a host of teachers from different styles and systems, all with different approaches and varying levels of knowledge and skill. The end result is that they come away very confused, with an assortment of unenviable 'skills' and an even greater collection of bad habits that may never be corrected. We see this as a sad waste of the time, interest and resources they have put into this enterprise. Had they spent longer with one good teacher, they may have penetrated the depths that they missed.

Then again, it can be very difficult to recognise a good teacher or to know whether or not what they are passing on is actually authentic Tai Chi. We sometimes hear from experienced Tai Chi practitioners who have gone along to a class that is advertised as Tai Chi and found that no Tai Chi was being taught there at all. In some cases, it might just be a type of qigong; in other cases, a made up exercise system. Often, this is not the fault of the teacher, since they themselves have spent time and money learning these exercises in the belief that they were learning Tai Chi, and the same may be true of their own teacher, and theirs, going way back. We will assume that you have been lucky enough to have avoided this potential pitfall.

So, when you have you have succeeded in passing on your skills and knowledge to a student, how do you know when they are ready to teach, if they want to?

Traditionally, giving someone permission to teach infers not only that they have reached a particular level of skill but also that you are able to trust certain qualities of their character, such as their moral integrity, their intelligence and their ability to get on well with people.

It is obvious that a person who is impatient, aggressive, anti-social and uncaring would not be the kind of teacher you would be happy to release on an unsuspecting public!

Fortunately, the nature of Tai Chi makes it unlikely that such a person would have the patience to reach a high level of skill in the first place, though they might, in their own mind, believe themselves to be a master of the art!

In our experience, we have found that Tai Chi tends to attract people who are peace-loving, kind and interested in exploring the deeper mysteries of life. The ability to stick with it long enough to learn a form requires patience, dedication and intelligence. It has been our privilege to have known thousands of such people and to have supported many of them as they developed into brilliant teachers.

In the end, you will use your own judgement as to whether or not you are happy to endorse a person as a teacher. You will have come to know them very well over the years and you will sense, from their attitude towards assisting their fellow students in class, whether they have a genuine desire to help others or whether they are trying to impress you or are doing it 'under sufferance' while itching to get on with their own training instead.

On rare occasions, we have met individuals who have tried to almost bully us into giving them a qualification in the shortest time possible. They may have done a little Tai Chi with a different teacher and come to us 'already formed', thinking they are an expert yet entrenched in bad habits that they are unwilling to recognise or attempt to correct. Fortunately, this is an extremely rare occurrence. Most people with previous experience are very open to learning and some are already very skilled. Part of the art of teaching is to be able to recognise the abilities of a student who is already experienced and to be able to offer them guidance in how to move forwards on their journey. If they practice a different style that you know very little about, be honest enough to say so and recommend that they look elsewhere.

Helping People with Previous Tai Chi Experience

Helping experienced students requires tact and sensitivity. First, we make it a rule never to show disrespect towards a student's former teacher. When we look at the student's form, we accept that each teacher will be likely to have their own approach and interpretations, even within the same style. Their Tai Chi may not be the same as ours yet it may still be very good and there is no reason for the student to give up the things they have put so much time and effort into learning just for the sake of conforming with what we are doing and keeping us happy.

Secondly, we always need to bear in mind that it is impossible to judge a teacher by their student. If one of our own students, at an early stage in their training, were to demonstrate their fairly uncoordinated efforts to a teacher down the road who had never met us, we would hope that they would not assume that they were seeing a faithful rendition of what we are actually teaching. Only a few students ever reach the stage where they could demonstrate their Tai Chi anywhere in the world without raising too many eyebrows - or face palms!

What we are judging, when we look at the existing Tai Chi skills of a newcomer, is how well what they are doing obeys the Tai Chi principles and we try to be helpful rather than critical.

It doesn't matter that they put in an extra roll-back or have a slightly different 'take' on how to repulse monkeys but it does matter that they are arching their back and sticking out their chest and bottom, or straining their knees, or leaning all over the place, or hunching their shoulders and pushing with arms as stiff as planks.

Even if their understanding of the principles is minimal and their Tai Chi is pretty awful, or not even actually Tai Chi, they have invested time and money in getting to where they are now and may be very proud of what they are doing. What we absolutely must not do is 'shoot them down in flames' at this point. We might think that we are simply being honest but our honesty could destroy their self-esteem and prevent them from gaining any further pleasure from studying Tai Chi.

So, when providing feedback, we try to always focus on what they are doing well and then offer suggestions to improve one thing at a time, beginning with the root and corrections of any major postural errors. Often a lot of other things will start to sort themselves out once these basics are addressed.

However, it is sometimes incredibly difficult to offer advice to a person whose Tai Chi is not following the principles if they are set in their ways and unwilling to change. Their loyalty to their previous teacher may be admirable, and they may be deriving intense pleasure from what they are doing, but to allow them to carry on doing it their way in your classes or, worse still, giving them a licence to teach it to others, would compromise your own integrity and do a disservice to your school and to Tai Chi in general.

In such cases, however polite, tactful, diplomatic and sensitive to their feelings we may try to be, the offering of any kind of suggestion for improvement, or even a less than ecstatic expression on our faces, is often interpreted as criticism and, sadly, guarantees that this person will not come back to us but will either give up Tai Chi, or find another teacher, or set up a class of their own anyway.

In complete contrast, we have also known rare and very special individuals whose humility and willingness to learn has allowed them to take some of our suggestions on board and take their skills to a very high level. In one case, we were astonished and humbled by a long-established teacher who was so willing to go on learning and developing her art that she actually gave us her own class and enrolled herself in it as our student! This lady is a truly great teacher whose courage, dignity and strength of spirit we can only aspire to. As we have so often said, teaching is a two-way process in which we can learn more from our students than they learn from us, and it isn't always about Tai Chi!

The Highest Levels

With patience, dedication and the right teacher, students may, at last, reach a stage where they can use their martial skills effortlessly without undue force or weakness. They may begin to experience what we referred to in Volume 1 as 'the mysterious IT'. Their movements may become perfectly timed, connected and coordinated, arising from deep within the dantien, directed by the waist and controlled by the power of intention.

Yin and yang, internal and external, force and energy, combine into the springy resilience and ease of movement that is the pure expression of Tai Chi. Although, their forms and skills at this level would allow them to compete in the international arena, they may no longer have a desire to prove anything.

Through meditation and the mindful practice of their art, they may eventually become their own master.

As we have said elsewhere, Tai Chi mastery is not about gathering knowledge as information, or the ability to demonstrate gymnastic feats or even the ability to defeat many opponents.

When someone becomes their own master, their understanding of the principles is so deep that they know instinctively when something feels right or not and they can self-correct any errors.

More importantly, they may become a master of their own mind so that they are no longer a slave to the emotions and addictions that can cause so much suffering and conflict in the world. Ironically, when someone reaches this stage, they may not consider themselves to be a master, because they will recognise that life is a continuing process in which there is always more to be learned, more to be experienced, more to be expressed.

At the highest levels, their forms and martial skills become spontaneous and their focus of attention can switch effortlessly between the local and the universal. With the mind resting in Wu Chi, Tai Chi becomes an expression of the universe and the individual practitioner dissolves into pure being experiencing itself.

We are always engaged in this process of discovery. In this way, we participate in the universal process of creation.

There is no end to it; no final point where you can say to yourself: "That's it! I've got it now! Time to put my feet up." Life goes on. Even when we give up the doing, there is still the being...until there isn't.

Epilogue

In writing this book, we have shared with you our own approach to teaching, based on our personal experience over several decades. We hope that it will not be one that you just read through and then put aside but that it will serve you as a helpful handbook that you can refer to many times, like a guide at your side, as you develop your skills as a teacher.

We don't consider ourselves to be experts or consider that our way is the only way to teach. There are many great teachers out there who will have found what works best for themselves and their students and they may not agree with everything we say. Like us, they may have post-graduate teaching qualifications and have been taught all the various theories of learning and yet, also like us, much of what they know will have been learned the hard way. That process is inevitable as, however much people try to standardise teaching, every teacher and every learner is a unique individual, as is every teaching environment. This is its strength, like the difference between a uniform crop of corn and a botanical garden or a rain forest.

We know that you will learn your greatest lessons as you go along, about your students and their needs, about what works for you and for them, and about yourself. Once you start to teach, your understanding of Tai Chi is likely to increase exponentially and we hope that, like us, you will find great joy in this process of discovery and mutual learning that inevitably takes place in a Tai Chi class.

Although we have not pulled any punches about the realities of teaching, we hope that this book has inspired you and helped to prepare you for most eventualities you might encounter so that, as well as being a great Tai Chi practitioner, you can now become a great Tai Chi teacher.

Whatever motivated you to become a teacher, whether you wanted to supplement your income, change your career or simply to provide a valuable service to others, we hope that you find great pleasure from teaching Tai Chi and that it enriches your life and the lives of those you teach in many ways, as it has for us and for our students.

This 7 Steps Towards Mastery series has, in many ways, been the fulfilment of our life's work, enabling us to achieve our ambition of leaving something worthwhile behind us for the next generation by passing our skills and knowledge on to you and to others like you. We believe that Tai Chi Chuan is not only one of China's greatest treasures but one of the world's greatest treasures. The fact that you have had the interest and the patience to read these words gives us hope that you will help us to keep this unique and invaluable martial art alive and carry the torch forwards into the future, and for this we thank you. We wish you a long and successful career as a Tai Chi teacher.

All the best, Colin and Gaynel, May 2018

Appendix 1

Suggested Needs-specific Learning Outline

Date Time Venue

Reminders / Resources needed

Warm Ups

New Starters

Beginners

Intermediate students

Advanced Students / Trainee Instructors

Qualified Instructors attending for Professional Development

Readings / Exercises / Discussions /Themes

Evaluation

Appendix 2

Suggested Initial Learner Agreement/Feedback Sheet

The following can be used at the start and end of a programme. Simply take a sheet of A4 paper, add a title: *Initial Learner Agreement and Feedback Sheet*, and then divide the rest of the page into two columns and copy the following list into each column under the headings:

Start of Programme.

I wish to study Tai Chi Chuan in order to:

and

End of Programme.

This Tai Chi programme has helped me to:

Then let your students write their initials at the top and then use the same sheet twice as a tick list – ticking options in the left hand column at the beginning of term/semester and in the right hand column at the end of term/semester. You may think of other things to add but the following are the motives and outcomes most frequently reported by our own (thousands of) students:

Improve my posture and balance

Improve my mobility

Improve my flexibility

Improve my co-ordination

Improve my health and fitness

Learn to relax and feel calmer

Meet people and make friends

Gain more confidence

Learn how to protect/defend myself

Sleep better

Feel happier

Gain a qualification in Tai Chi Chuan

My other specific aims/hopes/intentions are:

(Leave a space for them to insert these.)

At the bottom of the first column, you might have:

Please tick either (1) or (2)

(1) I had never done Tai Chi before starting this course. My aim this year is to learn a short Tai Chi sequence and understand the main principles of Tai Chi movement.

(2) I have previous Tai Chi experience. My aim this year is to improve/extend my skills and deepen my understanding of the art.

At the bottom of the second column, you might have:

Please tick all that apply:

I have now learned a short sequence of Tai Chi movements which I am able to practice on my own or when I follow others in a group.

I have improved my Tai Chi forms and learned more about the Tai Chi principles.

Other comments about what I have gained from the course / my plans for future learning:

When you find yourself with a pile of completed forms, you can easily add up the ticks for each item on the list and transfer the numbers anonymously to a spreadsheet in order to generate bar charts and diagrams showing what your students wanted and how well their aims and objectives were achieved. If you do this, put the charts into your teaching file to inform your future teaching. However, make sure that you tell your students why this information is being collected, what it will be used for and whom it might be shared with (such as inspectors). Keep the data anonymous and shred the forms as soon as you have finished with them.

References and Further Reading

Articles and Research Papers

Bond, Michael, *Ready for anything: The best strategies to survive a disaster*. New Scientist, (Online edition). 10th May 2017. https://www.newscientist.com/article/mg23431250-400-ready-for-anything-the-best-strategy-to-survive-a-disaster/

Bond, Michael, *How to Survive a Disaster*. BBC Future. http://www.bbc.com/future/story/20150128-how-to-survive-a-disaster

Fessler, D.M.T., Holbrook, C., *Marching into battle: synchronized walking diminishes the conceptualized formidability of an antagonist in men*. The Royal Society. Published 27 August 2014. DOI: 10.1098/rsbl.2014.0592
http://rsbl.royalsocietypublishing.org/content/10/8/20140592

Gais, S. *Sleep after learning aids memory recall*. Learning and Memory, 13, 259-262. (2006)
http://learnmem.cshlp.org/content/13/3/259.full.html

Klein, P.W., *Those who can't do, teach? Think again*, Contributed to The Globe and Mail, Published June 5, 2015. Updated March 25, 2017.
https://www.theglobeandmail.com/globe-debate/those-who-can-learn-certainly-do-teach/article24818663/

Maguire, E. A. et al, (2000) *Navigation-related structural changes in the hippocampi of taxi drivers*. Proceedings of the National Academy of Sciences of the United States of America, Volume 97, No.8, 4398-4403 doi: 10.1073/pnas.070039597.
http://www.pnas.org/content/97/8/4398

Maslow, A. H. (1943). A theory of human motivation. Psychological Review, 50(4), 370-396. APA PsycNet. American Psychological Association.
http://psycnet.apa.org/record/1943-03751-001 and
http://dx.doi.org/10.1037/h0054346

Merchant, J., *Mindfulness and meditation dampen down inflammation genes*. New Scientist, 16 June 2017
https://www.newscientist.com/article/2137595-mindfulness-and-meditation-dampen-down-inflammation-genes/

Mortimer, J.A., Ding, D., Borenstein, A.R., DeCarli, C., Guo, Q., Wu, Y, Zhao, Q., and Chu, S., *Changes in Brain Volume and Cognition in a Randomized Trial of Exercise and Social Interaction in a Community-Based Sample of Non-Demented Chinese Elders*. Journal of Alzheimer's Disease, Volume 30, Number 4, June 2012 Pages 757-766. http://www.j-alz.com/issues/30/vol30-4.html

Tunçgenç, B., and Cohen, E., *Movement Synchrony Forges Social Bonds across Group Divides*. Institute of Cognitive and Evolutionary Anthropology, School of Anthropology and Museum Ethnography, University of Oxford, Oxford, UK. Frontiers of Psychology, 27 May 2016 | https://doi.org/10.3389/fpsyg.2016.00782

Walker, Matthew. (2017) *Wake-up call: How a lack of sleep can cause Alzheimer's*. New Scientist, 14th October 2017 edition. https://www.newscientist.com/article/mg23631470-600-wake-up-call-how-a-lack-of-sleep-can-cause-alzheimers/

Wang, C., Schmidt, C.H., Fielding, R.A., et.al., *Effect of Tai Chi versus aerobic exercise for fibromyalgia*. British Medical Journal, 2018 360:k851.
http://dx.doi.org/10.1136/bmj.k851

Williams, C., How to extinguish the inflammation epidemic New Scientist, 14 June 2017
https://www.newscientist.com/article/mg23431300-500-how-to-extinguish-the-inflammation-epidemic/

Books

Tai Chi Classics, Waysun Liao, Shambhala, 1977. ISBN 0-87773-531-X. New Edition 2001. ISBN-10: 1570627495, ISBN-13: 978-1570627491

Advanced Yang Style Tai Chi Chuan Volumes 1 and 2, Dr. Yang, Jwing Ming, Yang's Martial Arts Association, 1986 Republished as: *Tai Chi Chuan Martial Power: Advanced Yang Style*. YMAA Publication Center; 3rd revised edition 16 April 2015. ISBN-10: 1594392943, ISBN-13: 978-1594392948

Tai Chi Touchstones: Yang Family Secret Transmissions, Douglas Wile, Sweet Ch'i Press, 1983. ISBN-10: 091205901X, ISBN-13: 978-0912059013

Lost T'ai-chi Classics from the Late Ch'ing Dynasty, Douglas Wile, Albany: SUNY, 1996. ISBN-10: 0791426548, ISBN-13: 978-0791426548

The Notebooks of Paul Brunton, Volume 2, *Overview of the Quest*, 4:3:111 Larson Publications. ISBN-0-943914-16-7 and 978-0-943914-16-9

Pearls of Wisdom, Dadi Janki. Health Communications (1 Sept. 1999).ISBN-10: 1558747230, ISBN-13: 978-1558747234

First Aid Manual, Revised 10th Edition 2016, St John Ambulance, St Andrew's First Aid and the British Red Cross. Dorling Kindersley Publishing. ISBN-978-0-2412-4123-3

Useful Organisations and Governing Bodies

The British Council for Chinese Martial Arts (BCCMA)
https://bccma.com/

The Tai Chi Union for Great Britain (TCUGB)
http://www.taichiunion.com/

The British Combat Association (BCA) Established by Peter Consterdine and Geoff Thompson.
http://britishcombat.co.uk/index.aspx

The Human Givens Institute. Established by Joe Griffin and Ivan Tyrell.
https://www.hgi.org.uk/human-givens

The Information Commissioner's Office (ico.) The UK's independent authority set up to uphold information rights in the public interest, promoting openness by public bodies and data privacy for individuals. This website gives clear guidance on current Data Protection regulations, including the new GDPO.
https://ico.org.uk/for-organisations/

Music Licences in the UK
https://pplprs.co.uk/themusiclicence/

By the Authors

Companion Volumes in the 7 Steps Towards Mastery Series

How to Move Towards Tai Chi Mastery: 7 Practical Steps to Improve your Tai Chi Forms and Access your Internal Power, Colin and Gaynel Hamilton, 2018. Paperback version ISBN: 9781980688921

How to Use Tai Chi for Self-defence: 7 Practical Steps to Develop Your Martial Skills and Avoid Having to Use Them, Colin and Gaynel Hamilton, 2018. Paperback version ISBN: 9781980688938

Magazine Articles

Hamilton, G., *Britain's Best Kept Secret?: An Interview with Master Zhu*, Tai Chi Chuan Magazine: The Journal of the Tai Chi Union for Great Britain, Issue 10, pages 38-41, 1998.

Hamilton, G., *A Circular Route to Tai Chi Mastery*, Tai Chi Chuan and Oriental Arts Magazine: The Journal of the Tai Chi Union for Great Britain, Issue 49, pages 24-26, 2015

Hamilton, G., *There Are No Secrets? Well, Actually…,* Tai Chi Chuan and Oriental Arts Magazine: The Journal of the Tai Chi Union for Great Britain, Issue 50, pages 44-45, 2016

Free eBooks for beginners (as downloadable pdf files):

Hamilton, G., *Your Tai Chi Companion Part 1: Getting Started.* Yiheyuan Martial Arts, 2009. http://www.taichileeds.com/

Hamilton, G., *Your Tai Chi Companion Part 2: Moving On.* Yiheyuan Martial Arts, 2012. http://www.taichileeds.com/

Made in United States
North Haven, CT
09 January 2022